GOD'S HEALING PROCESS

An Everyday State of Grace Existence

David Ian Copeland, Ph.D. LMHC-S

Copyright © 2022 David Ian Copeland, Ph.D. LMHC-S.

All rights reserved. No part of this book may be used or reproduced by any means, graphic, electronic, or mechanical, including photocopying, recording, taping or by any information storage retrieval system without the written permission of the author except in the case of brief quotations embodied in critical articles and reviews.

WestBow Press books may be ordered through booksellers or by contacting:

WestBow Press
A Division of Thomas Nelson & Zondervan
1663 Liberty Drive
Bloomington, IN 47403
www.westbowpress.com
844-714-3454

Because of the dynamic nature of the Internet, any web addresses or links contained in this book may have changed since publication and may no longer be valid. The views expressed in this work are solely those of the author and do not necessarily reflect the views of the publisher, and the publisher hereby disclaims any responsibility for them.

Any people depicted in stock imagery provided by Getty Images are models, and such images are being used for illustrative purposes only.
Certain stock imagery © Getty Images.

Unless otherwise indicated, all Scripture quotations are from the ESV® Bible (The Holy Bible, English Standard Version®), Copyright © 2001 by Crossway, a publishing ministry of Good News Publishers. Used by permission. All rights reserved.

Scripture marked (KJV) taken from the King James Version of the Bible.

ISBN: 978-1-6642-7644-4 (sc)
ISBN: 978-1-6642-7643-7 (hc)
ISBN: 978-1-6642-7645-1 (e)

Library of Congress Control Number: 2022915953

Print information available on the last page.

WestBow Press rev. date: 10/07/2022

First, I thank God for answering prayers, even when the answers were not comfortable or easy. A very special thanks to my wife, Dreeta, for her loving support, encouragement, and patience. I am also thankful for our family for their ongoing support on this journey, which included facing various trials along the way that challenged us all to the core of our faith.

Finally, special thanks to all my professors, military service members, and spiritual mentors over the years for their words of encouragement, guidance, and observations; each of them has always seemed to be at the right place and time.

CONTENTS

Preface ix

Chapter 1   Beginnings 1
Chapter 2   Darkness Revealed: Living as an Emotional Pain Carrier ... 18
Chapter 3   The Unfortunate Epiphany; Being an Emotional
                  Pain Carrier 22
Chapter 4   The Greater Hope 30
Chapter 5   Grow Beyond the Known 42
Chapter 6   Coming Out of the Darkness 48
Chapter 7   A New Beginning 60
Chapter 8   Creation Therapy and GHP Theory Dynamic 67
Chapter 9   Dead-Ends and Detours 73
Chapter 10   An Examination of Refinement 79
Chapter 11   Worldwide Epidemics of Anxiety and Depression;
                  Post-Traumatic Stress 87

List of Figures 103
References 105

PREFACE

Questions can be an important part of our lives in making a discovery. This book is an observation that our lives are being refined by God. By utilizing what I have celebrated as God's healing process (GHP), we may have access to that which can give hope in determining the needed direction to apply for spiritual transformation. GHP theory is a practical way of meeting people where they are and helping them to transition into where God desires. GHP does this by helping identify patterns and potential problems and pitfalls that may have interfered or hindered mental, physical, and spiritual areas of health, well-being, and growth. Although I am enthusiastic about its potential, I have also noticed the challenges within individuals because GHP has a way of either waking or shaking them up to evaluate and be honest with themselves. Many have recognized where they are spiritually and decided to change; others have reacted to another extreme of anger and fear, yelling, "Are you telling me I am going to burn in hell?" When that happens, I ask them to be aware and notice that inward conviction taking place because there may be a need to change something in their lives. GHP's power to positively influence people has been surprising. In individual work with people, GHP has provided a direct recognition to help promote a need for positive change and direction in life. It is always the person's choice if they decide to recognize the need to change. GHP can be flexible in use and provide practical ways of reaching others who may have experienced maladaptive conversions or false religious beliefs that have led to the experience of what led some have called post-traumatic church disorder (PTCD). I hope that many will find this helpful in your journey as it has been in mine.

God's healing process is an on-growing work done by God. It occurs through us as we obey His Word and attune to His will. We become an extension of God's grace by not only accepting it but also fully receiving it within. The life we gain flows through us like living waters. Love begets love, grace begets grace, and faith begets faith.

God bless,
Dr. David I. Copeland, PhD, LMHC-S

– 1 –
Beginnings

Everyone has a way of escaping the pain they experience in life, because pain, whether emotional or physical, is not pleasant. The escape pattern a person develops can be going into a fantasy world (virtual reality) and engaging in other means of self-medication. Self-medicating is not limited to misused pharmacy medication or illicit drugs; it is the use of anything to numb, disassociate, or escape current circumstances. An individual can get by using productive or destructive ways. Continued use of substances or patterns can lead to addictive behaviors because the body builds up a tolerance. The body has a balance, and with everything a person takes in, the body adjusts. So, if a chemical is put into the body, the normal production of the chemicals (dopamine, oxytocin, etc.) is reduced to keep the body balanced. When the chemicals a person puts in their body stop abruptly, the body regears itself to reproduce the lost amounts, and a person can feel withdrawal symptoms.

The idea of battling addiction begins with different personal experiences, observations, and approaches. But how are addictions formed? What is the purpose behind the behavior? While developing an understanding of addictive behavior, having a realistic evaluation of personal experiences can be important. Experiences are foundational to developing survival techniques and creating a belief of the world around us. Your approach to helping people with addictions will follow your belief system. Because foundational beliefs influence the way individuals apply tools for helping people, gaining a deeper understanding of the biblical views of addictions may aid us in establishing a more accurate and holistic approach for applied grace. Word searches on the biblical use of the terms related to counseling and addictions may help provide a foundation for an integrative approach. The cross-examination of the Word searches may show many similarities of known practice and applications of addiction treatment, however differences that exist may be compared. This is not a comprehensive examination but only a general overview.

> All Scripture is breathed out by God and profitable for teaching, for reproof, for correction, and for training in righteousness, that the man of God may be competent, equipped for every good work. (2 Timothy 3:16–17 ESV)

He is the Creator (Genesis 1:1) and foundation of the world (Psalm 102:25); all authority and wisdom are from Him. There are many options to derive knowledge to help someone with addictive behaviors. However, all the theories, treatment plans, and diagnoses made may not actually be beneficial for all individuals. The sufficiency of God has been questioned because of an intellectualization of the scripture. Without the practical application of scripture, there is no gaining of experience or building of faith. Without experience or building of faith, there is no spiritual growth.

The shields of survival generated by the genius of the brain from historic trauma create voids. These unperceived voids are the unknown. The darkness of the unknown is sustained by fear; the needed avoidance of pain is based on fear of going through it again. Once light enters darkness, an opportunity to heal may be realized. However, the over-intellectualization of God's Word strains out the gnat and swallows the camel (Matthew 23:24). Without gained experience (application), humankind's plans are substituted for God's will, leading to chaos. Proverbs 19:21 (ESV) says, "Many are the plans in the mind of a man, but it is the purpose of the LORD that will stand."

The purpose of this section is to develop a deeper understanding of biblical views of counseling and addiction and how they compare with current and historical professional views. An examination of scripture will reveal key truths that lay a biblical foundation for Christian counselors in their professional duties. A study of counseling and addiction terms in the Bible will be expounded upon, and then based on this foundation, a comparison will be made between biblical and professional views of counseling and addiction. Finally, a discussion will be given of the impact of this knowledge on my professional and personal life.

BIBLICAL TERMS RELATED TO COUNSELING

A study of counseling-related words in the Bible was conducted. Using a Bible concordance, the terms were identified in their original Hebrew (Old Testament) and Greek (New Testament) language. The words were defined from Bible dictionaries and lexicons. Observations were made of the number of times the Hebrew and Greek words were translated, identification of any patterns of usage, and the range of meaning of the terms. Then, using Bible commentaries, scriptures from both the Old and New Testament were identified that illustrate what a biblical view of counseling includes.

Several terms were investigated, including *counsel*, *wisdom*, *help*, and *advice*. Using *Strong's Concordance* numbers for the Hebrew and Greek translations, a search was made in the lexicon and other dictionaries. This was accomplished through an online Bible study tools program.

Counsel

The English word *counsel* appears 143 times in scripture, and it has eight derivatives translated from Hebrew and four derivatives from Greek (Blue Letter Bible 1996). It appears as a verb meaning "to receive counsel or to take counsel" (Vine 1985, 246). As a noun, it refers to a counselor or those who give counsel (Vine 1985).

Old Testament Usage

In the Old Testament, *counsel* is translated from eight different Hebrew words. The most common translation is the Hebrew word *ya'ats* (*Strong's* number 3289). It occurs eighty times in the Old Testament. As a verb, it is defined as "to advise or to counsel" (Vine 1985). It is first used in scripture when Jethro says to Moses (his son-in-law), "I will give thee counsel and God will be with thee" (Exodus 18:19 KJV). Another word derived from *ya'ats* is the Hebrew word *'etsah* (*Strong's* number 6098). When used in 1 Kings 12, Rehoboam, son of the wise Solomon, was becoming king of Judah and sought counsel regarding a political matter from two groups of advisors. First, counsel was sought from his elders, who advised him to be subject to his people so they in turn would support his reign. The younger group of advisors gave him counsel that was pleasing to the young king and adversely affected Rehoboam's future. In this situation, the best counsel was to deny one's pride and serve those under oneself, certainly a principle Jesus taught with his life. The foolish counsel was to please oneself at any cost. Based on biblical principles, counsel should not be given just to please another person with pretty words but to point them to the truth, even if that is difficult to hear.

New Testament Usage

The Greek word for *counsel* is *sumboulos* (*Strong's* number 4825) and is derived from the Greek root word *boulouo* (*Strong's* number 1011). The meaning is "to take counsel" (Blue Letter Bible 1996). In Luke 14:31, Jesus tells of a king who was well advised to consider the cost of going to war. This parable indicates the importance of receiving counsel before making a critical decision and considering the cost associated with the situation. Do you take counsel into consideration? If so, from whom do you seek counsel?

Wisdom

Wisdom appears 234 times throughout scripture. *Easton's Bible Dictionary* defines it as a "moral rather than an intellectual quality. To be foolish is to be godless. True wisdom is a gift from God to those who ask it" (Easton 2007). Wisdom is also described as a divine person: "Christ the power of God and the wisdom of God" (1 Corinthians 1:24 ESV). It is translated from ten different Hebrew words and two Greek words. The majority of occurrences are in Job, Psalms, Proverbs, and Ecclesiastes; therefore, these books are known as "wisdom literature" (Vine 1985, 290).

Old Testament Usage

The most frequently translated term from Hebrew is *chokmah* (*Strong's* number 2451). It is used 149 times throughout the Old Testament and refers to wisdom, experience, and shrewdness (Vine 1985). The first uses of the term are in Exodus and refer to the wisdom and abilities given by God to the workers of the tabernacle. "He hath filled him with the spirit of God, in wisdom, in understanding, and in knowledge, and in all manner of workmanship" (Exodus 35:31 ESV). It is important for one to remember that wisdom comes from God, and He enables each person to accomplish their tasks in their personal and professional life. If an individual acknowledges the call of God in their life, reliance on the wisdom of God is vital.

Chokmah is also the knowledge and ability to make right choices, which lead to maturity (Vine 1985). Before you can develop maturity, you must have the fear of the Lord. "The fear of the Lord is the beginning of knowledge: but fools despise wisdom and instruction" (Proverbs 1:7 ESV). The biblical principle is to fear the Lord; this leads to wisdom. Conversely, a foolish person despises wisdom and instruction.

New Testament Usage

Wisdom is translated from two Greek words, *sophia* (*Strong's* number 4678) and *phronesis* (*Strong's* number 5428). "While sophia is theoretical, phronesis is practical" (Vine 1985, 678). The theoretical wisdom involves the revelation of Christ as wisdom. Colossians 2:3 (ESV) states Christ is the one "in whom are hidden all the treasures of wisdom and knowledge." The Colossian Christians were being persuaded by false teaching that they should seek after wisdom, but not the wisdom from Christ. While it is not wrong to seek after wisdom and knowledge, it must be done in and through Christ (Guzik 2006a). This is an excellent example for the biblical view of counseling. It is not wrong to pursue knowledge in the professional area, but it is important to keep the perspective that all wisdom and knowledge is in Christ.

Help

The word *help* appears 126 times in scripture. It has eight Hebrew and ten Greek derivatives and represents a large variety of words. The

International Standard Bible Encyclopedia describes *help* as that which brings aid, support, or deliverance (Orr 2007).

Old Testament Usage

The most frequently used Hebrew term for *help* is *azar* (*Strong's* number 5826), along with the corresponding nouns *ezer* and *ezrah*. Azar is represented in Psalm 121:2 (ESV): "My help comes from the LORD, who made heaven and earth." The God described in this verse is not just God but Yahweh, who made heaven and earth. He is the only true and living God, the Creator. As one serves God, it is important to remember His power. Often we can be overwhelmed by the problems and difficulties in life and fail to realize the great power of God. Remembering the greatness of God we can trust in His power to overcome (Smith 2005). It is so vital to have this perspective when working in the helping profession. Situations for the professional can become burdensome and without the biblical view of Yahweh as our helper life can be difficult. This is also true for individuals as they face what is driving their addictive behaviors.

New Testament Usage

There are ten different forms of the Greek word translated for *help*. The meanings have slightly different variations, including a laying hold of, aid, to take instead of, to assist, and to cooperate (Vine 1985). The Greek word *sunantilambano* (Strong's number 4878) means to take hold with at the side for assistance (Vine 1985). Interestingly *sunantilambano* is the combination of three Greek words. When it is broken down, the first part is *sun*, which means "to do something in conjunction with someone else." The second part is *anti*, which means "against." The third part of the word is *lambano*, which means "to take" or "to receive." Notice these three words, when joined, forming a new word, *sunantilambano*, which means to take hold of something with someone, grabbing hold of it, and putting the combined weight to move it out of the way. This is reflective of the ministry of the Holy Spirit when we are weak. Romans 8:26 (ESV) states, "Likewise the Spirit helps us in our weakness. For we do not know what to pray for as we ought, but the Spirit himself intercedes for us with groanings too deep for words." Notice the biblical view of help can be comforting and strengthening for individuals as they face personal weaknesses.

Advice

The word *advice* appears nine times in Scripture. There are five Hebrew derivatives and one Greek derivative. The International Standard Bible Encyclopedia describes *advice* as "to request or to consult with oneself" (Orr 2007).

Old Testament Usage

Of the five Hebrew derivatives, all but one is translated the same as *counsel*. *Ta' am* (Strong's number 2940) is used in 1 Samuel 25:33, where David becomes violently angry but listens to the advice of Abigail, which prevents him from committing sin. David, the king, was willing to receive advice at an emotionally charged time in his life from one of his own people. One would do well to follow this example.

New Testament Usage

The Greek derivative for *advice* is *gnome* (Strong's number 1106) and is translated nine times in the New Testament. It means "an opinion, purpose, judgment," (Vine 2007). It is also related to the Greek word for *purpose*. During the early Church, the apostles were brought to the Jewish council and questioned by the high priest because they had told them to stop preaching Christ (Acts 5). Gamaliel (a teacher of the law) advised the council not to go against these men (Acts 5:35–39 ESV), "'but if it is of God, you will not be able to overthrow them. You might even be found opposing God!' So, they took his advice." The point made by this teacher was that if it is of God, you cannot stop what is going on.

Biblical Terms Related to Addiction

The same format for studying counseling terms was used for addiction terms in the Bible. The terms investigated include *wine, strong drink, self-control,* and *abstinence.*

Wine

The English word *wine* appears 231 times in Scripture, and it has eleven derivatives translated from Hebrew and five derivatives from Greek (Blue Letter Bible 1996). *Easton's Bible Dictionary* defines it as "to tread out, hence the juice of the grape trodden out" (Easton 2007). The Hebrew word *tirosh* (Strong's number 8492) has been traced to a root meaning "to take possession of," and therefore it is associated with intoxicating as it takes possession of the brain (Easton 2007).

Old Testament Usage

The most frequently translated term from Hebrew is *yayin* (Strong's number 3196). It is used 140 times throughout the Old Testament and refers to bubbling up and fermenting. It first occurs in Genesis 9:21 when Noah was overcome with wine (Blue Letter Bible 1996). Noah's own actions show the foolishness of drunkenness and are opposite of the filling of the Holy Spirit referred to in Ephesians 5:18, which states one should not get drunk with wine but be filled with the Spirit (Guzik 2006). However, it is also interesting to note that Noah did not have access to the Holy Spirit because Jesus had not sent it out until He ascended. Also, Noah's behavior was influenced by being a witness to the destruction of humankind by the flood.

New Testament Usage

Onios (Strong's number 3631) is a general word for *wine* and includes the bursting of the wineskins (Vine 1985). The apostle Paul points toward abstinence because the drinking of wine can be a stumbling block for others (Romans 14:21). Another usage of wine, *gleukos* (Strong's number 1098), is in Mark 14:25 when Jesus initiates the Lord's Supper and speaks of the contents of the cup as wine. Wine can be used in a holy way or in a destructive manner. Each person must determine their level of participation and their reasons for or against participating in drinking wine. When an individual evaluates their reasons for any addictive behaviors, what may be discovered is a pattern of avoidance and dissociation out of fear. The problem avoided is still there with a delayed decaying situation that exists. Living in fear leads to sin and ultimately to death.

STRONG DRINK

The exact term of *strong drink* is translated nineteen times in Scripture, and it occurs in the Old Testament. There are many derivatives from Hebrew and Greek for the separate terms *strong* and *drink*, but an evaluation is made for the combined words *strong drink*.

Old Testament Usage

The only translation of *strong drink* in the Old Testament is *shekar* (Strong's number 7941), meaning an intoxicant, intensely alcoholic liquor (Vine 2007). It is used three times in Proverbs and refers to the destruction caused by drunkenness. There are consequences of such behavior that makes a person appear as a fool and unfit for society and outrageous in his or her passions (Henry 1996b). It is also used in Isaiah 5:22 as a warning that men who get drunk abuse their bodily strength that God has given them for good purposes. It is a sin that will make them vulnerable to the wrath and curse of God (Henry 1996c). The biblical view of strong drink shows the unpleasantness of sinful behavior and why it should be avoided.

SELF-CONTROL

The term *self-control* is translated as *temperance* in the King James Version of the Bible and is used four times in the New Testament. The Greek word is *egkrateia* (Strong's number 1466) and means "the virtue of the one who masters his desires and passions, especially his sensual appetites" (Thayer n.d.).

New Testament Usage

Temperance is listed as a part of the fruit of the Spirit in Galatians 5:23. While the world understands that self-control is for a selfish reason, representing the self-discipline and denial a person goes through for themselves, the self-control of the Spirit will work on behalf of others (Guzik 2006b). The Apostle Paul uses the phrase *fruit of the Spirit* in a singular form, indicating there is a cluster of fruit where all the qualities are manifested in every believer (Guzik 2006b). This is important in addiction counseling to identify that every person has the fruit of self-control, but some may need more help to exercise that quality by grace and faith. Ultimately, it is the God's working through the Holy Spirit within a person that provides the ability to heal by refinement. So how does that take place?

Because the working of the Holy Spirit provides a potential for strength or resilience, it works only to the amount of an individual's belief system and their willingness become refined. What keeps people from being willing to be refined is fear. What type or kind of fear? Here is a brief list, but notice what fear may exist within you.

> Fear of being in painful events, or going through painful events again
> Fear of rejection
> Fear of abandonment
> Fear of being discovered for their behavior
> Fear of losing their addictive support system
> Fear of change
> Fear of the unknown

ABSTINENCE

The term *abstinence* is from the root *abstain*, derived from the Greek word *apecho* (Strong's number 568), and it means to hold oneself from, referring to evil practices or moral and ceremonial acts (Vine 1985). It is used six times in the New Testament.

New Testament Usage

All six usages refer to holding oneself back from evil practices or fleshly lusts, which include drinking strong drinks and becoming drunk. In 1 Peter 2:11, Peter warns believers to abstain from fleshly lusts that war against the soul. As long as a believer lives in the flesh, there will be a war against fleshly lusts (Guzik 2006c). Addiction counseling can emphasize that the battle against the desire for the addictive behavior will be a continuous struggle for the person. The power of the Holy Spirit to overcome addiction is possible, but the person must be connected to God and submit their fleshly desires or escape patterns to the Spirit. If a lamp has all the working parts to make light but is never plugged into an electrical outlet, it will never produce light. No matter how many times you turn the switch, change the bulb, clean the socket, dust the lampshade, or move it to a different part of the room, unless the lamp is plugged into the electrical outlet, it simply will not work.

Based on the word study of counseling and addiction terms in the Bible, a review of addiction counseling literature was performed to compare and contrast biblical views with professional views. There are numerous conceptual models for treating addictive problems such as a disease model, moral model, spiritual model, biological model, educational model, cognitive model, and public health model. Treatment outcome research supports neither a singular model approach nor an uncritical eclecticism approach; in fact, evidence supports the use of various empirically supported options (Hester and Miller 2003). Gaining an understanding of a biblical approach as well as professional approaches will be in the best interest of the individual. First similarities will be discussed between the two views, and then differences will be examined.

Similarities between Biblical and Professional Views of Addiction Counseling

In research using concept mapping conducted by Neff, Shorkey, and Windsor (2006), traditional substance abuse treatment programs share several key dimensions with faith-based programs. Seven dimensions were examined, resulting in four with similarities and three with differences between the approaches. Similarities include the dimensions of "safe, supportive environment" and "role modeling and mentoring," explained as treatments allow for a warm, supportive environment, letting the individual know they are accepted, providing for basic needs, and encouraging role modeling of healthy recovery including testimonials of spirituality. The "role model and mentoring" dimension also includes using recovering staff workers as models and daily recreation as opportunities for modeling to be strengthened.

The third similar dimension is "group activities and cohesion." The treatment group is seen as a family with regular group meetings, encouraged participation, and regular activities such as singing, music, and drama (Neff et al. 2006). Professional approaches, as well as biblically based or faith-based programs, capitalize on the group cohesion and the social integration offered in the group setting. The fourth dimension that both approaches share is "traditional treatment modalities." In the research from Neff et al. (2006), the faith-based programs offered detoxification services, drug and alcohol education, and Alcoholics Anonymous (AA) or Celebrate Recovery (CR) meetings. Not all biblically based programs will offer such a variety of services, but the programs in Neff et al. (2006) included them.

Similarities between biblical and professional views also include basic counseling considerations. Addictive behaviors in which people struggle are the same (Bufford 1997). Whether Christian or non-Christian people experience problems, research indicates little difference in the rate of substance use regardless of church attendance of any denomination (Dyslin 2008). Because "all have sinned and fall short of the glory of God" (Romans 3:23 ESV), people will struggle with difficulties. Also, many of the intervention strategies and techniques are similar between both viewpoints. "These include emphasis on the importance of the counseling relationship, providing support and confrontation, and making cognitive and behavioral interventions" (Bufford 1997, 118). It is important to have an understanding and keep in mind that everyone is different and has their own life experience. Remember, they are the best expert for themselves. In other words, if you are looking for the best reference book to refer to treat an individual, look to that person. The person is their own frame around which, their personal experience of life is held.

Differences between Biblical and Professional Views of Addiction Counseling

Neff et al. (2006) report three dimensions that are clear differences between the faith-based and traditional programs. The first dimension is spiritual activities, beliefs, and rituals explained as using the Bible as a guide for behavior, providing regular Bible study, encouraging spiritual rather than material values, encouraging public affirmation of faith, and providing regular scripture reading. These activities were not observed in the treatment programs of the traditional approaches. The second dimension, work readiness and referral, was scored as significant in traditional programs but reported as insignificant in faith-based programs. This dimension is explained by the emphasis placed on the importance of work, providing job training, giving referrals to legal and medical services, and providing referrals to job counseling and job placement agencies.

The third dimension that is reported as being different between the faith-based and traditional programs is structure and discipline. The dimension is reported as significant for faith-based programs and much less important for traditional programs. It is described by penalties for rule violations, prohibits drug talk, prohibits cursing, and emphasizes respect for others. This follows a biblical view of loving the sinner but hating the sin.

Neff et al. identify other research that supports the dimensions of a warm and supportive environment within both secular and faith-based approaches. Christians have an opportunity to reflect a biblical love for a person as shown in agape love and providing a warm, accepting therapeutic relationship. Along with the agape love foundation, the structure and discipline can be used to help the individual develop more Christlike behaviors. This reflects a more complete biblical framework for addiction counseling.

Another difference not reported in the dimensions but included in the research data is the degree of training for the staff workers utilized in the treatment programs (Neff et al., 2006). Traditional programs used more professional, licensed staff than less formal faith-based programs, which used more unlicensed, nonprofessional staff. Many of the faith-based programs using the twelve-step–oriented treatments recruited staff members who are in recovery. Their level of training, though effective in some aspects of the treatment process, is much less than the professionals in the traditional programs.

People exhibiting addictive behaviors choose the recovery program that reflects their fundamental views, but a biblical approach should represent the concept of shalom: "God's intended state of whole and ordered righteousness for the people" (Miller 1995, 84). This is the theological context of the Presbyterian Church's statement on alcohol and drug use (cited in Miller 1995). Addictive behaviors place an individual in a state where they do not experience shalom and are at risk for potential harm to their bodies. The concept of shalom means more than just peace or an absence of war. It is inward tranquility and wholeness for an individual. When attachment issues and or trauma occur, it disrupts that inward peace. Broadening the inclusion of shalom allows for society's shared responsibility to address the problem of substance abuse and dependency.

Miller and Kurtz (1994) detailed the differences between the faith-based AA model and other traditional models such as moral-volitional, personality, and dispositional disease models. The moral-volitional model asserts that drunkenness is a choice for each person, and it leads to a lack of moral judgment. The personality model proposes that alcoholism is a result of an underlying personality disorder. But where does the personality disorder really come from? The dispositional disease model claims that chronic drunkenness is a disease leading the alcoholic to bear no responsibility for the development of the problem. Although some concepts of AA have often been confused with these traditional models, Miller and Kurtz (1994) delineate some differences. AA points out that the primary cause of alcoholism is a spiritual problem, not just a moral problem; it is an illness, the person exhibits some character flaws (not a disease model or personality disorder), and the source of healing comes from God (not medicine or psychotherapy).

A final difference is the use of spiritual surrender and interpersonal confession in the biblical treatment of addictive behaviors (Dyslin 2008). Spiritual surrender is the willingness to let go of living for self-centered desires and accepting one's limitations of human power and acknowledging the ultimate source of power in God through Jesus Christ. In the act of confession, one's pride is broken down, and the individual becomes a vessel for God's grace to be experienced. Both techniques are an integral concept of the faith-based programs AA, CR, and Steps to Freedom in Christ.

In my experience, there have been several individuals who have gone through these steps and found them to be unsuccessful. They go through the motions of programs or church patterns without finding or experiencing closure or freedom from the pain within. Instead of having a peaceful thriving, they enter a world of survival or "one day at a time" existence. Yet there are some who are successful in different programs as well. Is that success based upon a ritual process developed to help them feel good if they are working the program? If so, where is the working of God?

The role of a Christian is to reflect Christ's great commandment to love one another (Matthew 22:39) as he loved us (John 3:16). Therefore, it is important to love the individual seeking help. This love, created through God's healing process, produces an avenue to biblically help people experiencing cyclative behaviors and guide them through the power of the Holy Spirit, who can help break the cycle of pain through God's healing process. Noted in the word study section, *help* is translated from Greek and means to take hold with at the side for assistance (Vine 1985). Jesus sent the Holy Spirit as a helper when he left Earth (John 14). As we are in alignment with God, the indwelling of the Holy Spirit guides us in productive ways. In that way, God works through us, connecting and healing both the helper and those being helped. It is not the individual who is doing the work but the connection being brought to the individual in the moment through Christ. As an ambassador for Christ, this connection can be made because it is a commission (co-mission) with God.

Development of deep personal faith, counseling with excellence, holding to a biblical view, choosing treatment goals and techniques consistent with biblical truth, and actively seeking the presence and power of God will be evident in practice (Bufford 1997). Developing personal faith comes from applying Scripture in an appropriate way. It can bring transformational power because of the alignment it creates, by letting God work through you. As God's Word became flesh (Jesus) and dwelt among us, acknowledgment is made that Christ is "in whom are hidden all the treasures of wisdom and knowledge" (Colossians 2:3 ESV). The wisdom obtained increases faith for the authority for daily life is recognized by living out this truth of God's healing process daily. Renewing our minds in Christ is not meant to be an intellectualized endeavor but experiential. An everyday state of grace existence may be achieved, but it begins with each person.

God calls people to serve Him with excellence, as working unto the

Lord (Colossians 3:23). This idea has been used by some to shame and guilt people into better behavior or servitude toward others, but that is putting the cart before the horse. The idea of the word *heartily* (or *excellence*) in Colossians 3:23 is more aligned with the place of the Spirit. Individuals who are truly in alignment and attunement with God do not need to be coerced, thereby creating an environment of excellence. Those who instigate the need for forced obedience by fear are put in bondage and lord over people outside of God's design for reconciliation.

When serving others, it may be helpful to learn techniques from traditional modalities. When an individual has a biblical worldview, techniques from traditional modalities can be applied for the benefit of those being helped. Presence and curiosity help to gain Godly insight to best discern what tools and techniques are true for that individual. Misapplied tools may result only in further maladaptive behavior and continued addictive behaviors. It has been observed that counsel may be rejected by individuals who want to find an easier way to make changes without changing. The biblical example of Reboboam (1 Kings 12), highlighted in the word study section of this book shows that some people will choose to refuse Godly counsel or advice. People prefer the familiar, even when it is not working, rather than make a change. Making a choice to study and meditate on God's Word helps maintain cohesiveness in God's work being done in your life.

As a result of the research review for this section, it can be overwhelming to consider the complexities presented in the number of traditional and biblical approaches to addiction counseling. Continued education in different approaches is important to meet people where they exist in the present moment. Most individuals will come to counseling with an understanding of the approach the treatment will take. Informed consent will be provided to the individual by explaining the integrated biblical approach. It is important for individuals to be aware of what values will guide and shape the counseling process (Zinnbauer and Pargament 2000). Due to limitations, it is good to consider the use of detoxification facilities, medical facilities, and support groups such as AA or CR for the individuals needing to maximize results by expanding their overall support system.

Personal Implications to Consider

Overall, the quick study of addiction counseling has left a deeper understanding that we are all sinners in need of salvation. But what does that really mean? One realization is we all have patterns that bring death (aka sin), and we need structure that brings and gives life. Helping a person see their own need for God's power and grace may enable them to begin the process of being set free from the bondage of the addiction because deeper healing is able to take place.

Finally, the word study for the biblical usage to the term *abstinence* refers to 1 Peter 2:11 (ESV), which says one must "abstain from fleshly lusts that war against the soul." Any addictive behaviors (alcohol, drugs, or other destructive patterns) can be a continuous power struggle between the flesh and Holy Spirit. There is more than meets the eye when working with individuals and espousing them to submit their fleshly desire to the Holy Spirit; it is not likely to take place right away. It takes patience and grace as the individual grows. Those helping others need to examine themselves in their relationship to God through Christ, leaving darkness behind and entering the light. The greater stability modeled will help show the possibility that positive change can be attained and sustained.

— 2 —

Darkness Revealed: Living as an Emotional Pain Carrier

The addiction of the sinful nature leads to darkness. It is insidious and deceptive. Sadly, most individuals do not even recognize or know how or why it has happened.

Prior to becoming a full-time youth minister, I was in the United States Air Force for twenty years and had been deployed to many locations around the world. Wherever I was deployed, I always had my faith, and everywhere I went, there was always someone who was hurting and in some type of crisis. My faith was in action, and all that time, God was still working on me. While in the military, there were other ministry roles I served at a local congregation: deacon of the youth for four years, and deacon of evangelism for around five years.

After retiring from the USAF, I became a full-time youth minister. I noticed there were a lot more hurting families and people than realized. My preconceived idea about how I believed the church should be operating was brought to a hard reality check. The different capacities and capabilities of elders and ministers in ministering to others were less than expected. Although my expectations for professionalism and effectiveness within leadership roles and positions was disappointing, I still maintained the faith and belief in helping people with making effective change for good. God was working in me to grow, develop, and mature in Him. I noticed the different issues within families and began to look for better answers so I could be more effective as a youth minister. When I brought these different issues to light to the eldership, they deferred it from their role; their response was, "Let me know how that works out for you." It was very disappointing.

I began searching for more effective ways to minister and decided to go back to graduate school and take the full curriculum for becoming a marriage and family therapist (MFT) at an accredited university. I also desired to have a faith-based approach or Christian worldview because I believed it would be a great asset as a youth minister working for a congregation. Along the journey, I came across a program called Searching for Truth (SFT) Awareness, which caught my attention as a way of helping families and individuals. Ron Wilkins, the founder of the SFT Awareness program, promoted that there is the behavioral cycle or pain cycle (Wilkins 2006; see Fig. 1), and 98 percent of people are emotional pain carriers. I was intrigued, and after I completed the program for myself, I became a certified trainer and began working with individuals. What I discovered about myself was that I was not doing as well in my spiritual growth as I believed. Having to acknowledge that was bittersweet, but it was okay because it also affirmed Hebrews 11:6 (ESV), "And without faith it is impossible to please him, for whoever would draw near to God must believe that he exists and that he rewards those who seek him." This verse prompted me to question, Am I really seeking God and being blessed by the rewards He gives in my life?

As I introduced the SFT concept to individuals, I noticed that many made comments such as, "That's my life. How did you know?" People recognizing how it resembles their own life allows them to decide whether or not to do something about it. (Note: There are many examples of general behavior cycles, but I will be using the pain cycle that was developed and described by Ron Wilkins in his book *Removing Emotional Pain*; see Fig. 1.)

Some individuals recognize the effects of the problem(s) they are going through and seek to find a resolution. The SFT Awareness program is good at helping people come to deal with these issues in what I would call "taking every thought captive" (2 Corinthians 10:3–5 ESV). The techniques people are trained to use in the program help with breaking down those unbeknownst strongholds and reveal that they have systematically carried throughout their lives. Jesus told us that He came to give life more abundantly (John 10:10), but upon examining the evidence around people's lives, few seem to find it (Matt 7:14). Is having that type of peace is possible? Does God give us those keys in His Word to achieve that peace that surpasses understanding?

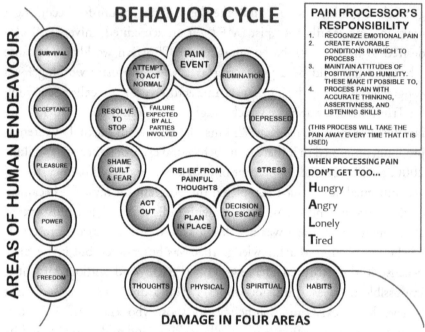

Figure 1. Behavioral cycle (Wilkins 2006)

During the time when Jesus was being tempted by Satan, Jesus confronted the lies by speaking the truth and taking an assertive action by using God's Word (Matthew 4). Having a way of taking every thought captive is important to being able to grow spiritually. It is important to rightly divide the Word of truth for proper understanding; otherwise, an individual will become delusional in their thought process. If we walk in darkness and are being deceived because of the rule of primacy, then the ability to choose to do something new becomes very challenging. For clarity's sake, the rule of primacy states what you learn first remains the longest. If you are taught or learn something incorrectly, it takes longer to retrain or change.

Religious traditions of humans keep people in darkness and prisoners to self-righteousness: they condemn others and justify themselves, believing they are doing God's will. Jesus stated these people will not enter into heaven (Matthew 7:21–23). God's state of being and our state of being is bridged only through what Jesus did for us, in Jesus Christ alone; that is, nothing (no thing) and no one else could ever have accomplished the reconciliation of God and humankind.

As I was teaching the class, I recognized that my previous ideas about people hurting and going through painful circumstances were at an epidemic proportion. I noticed the SFT Awareness approach was problematic because individuals with anxiety issues or living in survival mode are not focused on completing homework assignments. How can we help people take every thought captive and conform it to the mind of Christ when they are not able to be in their right mind?

The addiction of the sinful nature leads to darkness. It is insidious and deceptive. Sadly, most of us do not know how or why it has happened. Knowing is an important part of overcoming different challenges. However, we are limited by what we know and have experienced. Because we can do only what we know in the natural human, it takes faith to move beyond what we know and courage to not turn back into darkness. But how do we get there?

— 3 —

The Unfortunate Epiphany; Being an Emotional Pain Carrier

Like everyone else in the world, I thought I was doing all right. But when the truth of the matter was presented, I faced my reality and had to make a personal choice. It was ironic that while seeking out a way of helping others, I discovered the truth, and it was something troubling and humbling. What was it? I am an emotional pain carrier. I could intellectualize the passage "for all have sinned and fallen short of the glory of God" (Romans 3:23 ESV), but I was "okay," or so I thought. I could either stay in the emotional pain cycle or learn how to get freedom from it. I chose to be honest with myself and make changes accordingly to be right with my relationship with Christ.

Ron Wilkins (2006) noticed that there are three main characteristics of an emotional pain carrier: self-pity, shifting responsibility, and dumping. How about a quick self-check? Be completely honest.

> Have you ever felt sorry for yourself?
> Have you ever blamed someone else for what you didn't get accomplished?
> Has the day been so stressful that you told everyone about how horrible things have been?

Then, my friend, you may be an emotional pain carrier! Wilkins believed that 98 percent of people in this world are emotional pain carriers, and I discovered I was one too.

What is interesting is recognizing our own habits and noticing others around us in everyday communication. This realization can also become compelling when we realize how rampant and pervasive it exists with everyone inside and outside different congregations. We have learned to believe thinking errors because we do not recognize their existence. Thinking errors have become true lies that affect our beliefs. If we believe and practice lies, how can we worship God? After all, Jesus said "But the hour is coming, and is now here, when the true worshipers will worship the Father in spirit and truth, for the Father is seeking such people to worship him. God is spirit, and those who worship him must worship in spirit and truth" (John 4:23–24 ESV).

Hidden in plain sight, our deceptions or delusions (2 Thessalonians 2:9–12) may continue unless we remain diligent in seeking after God (Hebrews 11:6). Our examples around us in life while growing up and other multimedia sources are filled with thinking errors and reinforce and expand our false beliefs. Self-righteousness can hide in comfort until it is exposed by the light of the truth. Let us look at how the cycle starts.

EMOTIONAL PAIN CARRIER CYCLE

Pain Event

The pain cycle all starts with experiencing a pain event. A pain event is defined as anything that you don't like. Pain events are subjective to an individual's experience and can range from a 1 (low level) to 10 (top-level). A low-level event may be a simple annoyance like someone smacking gum. On the other side, an example of a top-level event would be of someone you love dying. Having a reaction is normal. An initial reaction to pain is arguably unstoppable. The basic idea is that pain events exist at all levels and when we are honest with ourselves (1 John 1:7–10) we can begin to respond instead of reacting in maladaptive ways in living life. But why are we reacting?

Rumination

After the pain event happens individuals think or talk about it repeatedly. This thought process is also known as rumination. Rumination is a choice that, if gone unchecked, continues to add to and continue the pain. The term rumination originally came from the digestive process of cows and was later applied to people who continued thinking about the past. Notice Peter's remarks in 2 Peter 2:22 (ESV). "What the true proverb says has happened to them: 'The dog returns to its own vomit, and the sow, after washing herself, returns to wallow in the mire.'" This description given by Peter is also reflected when looking at the whole Pain Cycle; a continued reoccurrence with individuals, without knowing how to stop. But what if we let God work through us to illicit true repentance, isn't it enough? Does God have a better plan in place? How do we attain His healing process?

Depression

Margaret Wehenburg (2016) noted that the process of rumination is a similarity between anxiety and depression. Basically, ruminating is simply repetitively going over and over a thought or a problem without completion. She noted that depressed people's ruminations are typically about being inadequate or worthless. Through repetition, feelings of inadequacy increase anxiety and anxiety interferes with solving the problem because the sympathetic side of the limbic system activates and interferes with cognitive processing. As a result, the depression cycle continues to deepen.

Stress

Stress for this illustration is going to be recognized and used as the negative context of anxiety. Wehenburg (2016) also stated that:

> Brain function plays a role in rumination in several ways, but one significant aspect of brain function relates to memory. People remember things that are related to each other in neural networks. And when people enter a 'woe is me' network the brain lights up connections to other times

they felt that way. Ruminating is worsened by another difficulty of the depressed and anxious brain: the inability to flexibly generate solutions. Brain chemistry makes it hard to switch to another perspective to find the way out of problems, so rumination intensifies. Both anxiety and depression are then reinforced. One interesting point is the negative thought process has been recognized and pinpointed to an area in the brain that sits next to the amygdala which is the predominant activation for the flight or fight mode. Science through SPECT scans has discovered that when this negative thought process begins it continues to stay active, creating and inducing anxiety.

Are we only to merely live and survive another day? Without Christ, from our own will, we are powerless. We are fearfully and wonderfully made (Psalms 139), even being wired with the ability to survive by God's design, but survival is not our intended end-state of existence. That is why Jesus came (John 10:10).

Decision to Escape

Without hope (Ephesians 2:12), individuals are faced with a never-ending repeat of pain events; the pressure continues to build to the point that they have a need to escape. Sadly, there are those people, including Christians, trapped living in this cycle for twenty, thirty, and even forty years! This pattern could be from learned helplessness. In general, learned helplessness is when a person has been conditioned to feel like they have no control over what happens, and they believe there is nothing they can do about anything. Don't worry because there is real help and hope. Remember the rule of primacy: you can only do what you know.

It is important to realize that whatever you are avoiding for the moment still exists, and that realization of not being fulfilled leads to becoming embittered and ultimately more pain events. One great example in the Bible is the Amnon and Tamar incident (2 Samuel 13). Notice that after Amnon's lust toward Tamar was filled by raping her, it turned to anger. The very thing we are driven by leads to more exasperation and futility, and helplessness and hopelessness are not far behind. But what is that driving force?

This list of escape behaviors is not exhaustive, but these behaviors can be recognized as anything used to bring relief from painful thoughts. Notice some escape behaviors help produce life, whereas others lead to death. Some say that there is a void or need that is looking to be filled that cannot be attained. However, in the work I have been doing, I notice an estimated 90 percent of people with addiction issues have a complex history of trauma stemming from early childhood. When individuals have experienced adverse childhood experiences (trauma), the addiction process is problematic and needs to be met in a different way. Remember, the genius of the brain to survive throughout different circumstances. It provides a system of reactance and alters behaviors needed to stay alive and survive. An individual's behaviors are born in reaction to events, to enable survival for another day. Being given the strength to survive allows an opportunity to come so healing can take place. As an individual discovers their patterns of life are maladaptive (not working), the cycle in which they exist is ready to be left behind. But for some reason, they are stuck and are unable to break free!

Plan in Place

From the first time after deciding to escape, an individual puts the plan in place. As this pattern goes on for some time, it develops into not just one plan; multiple backup plans are in place in case the first one fails. Each attempt to find release may or may not be considered because it is about finding relief from those painful thoughts. Addictive thinking becomes a life of its own, reacting to situations and feeding the need for more reactions. The ability to respond to life is further diminished with each passing cycle as the feelings of helplessness and hopelessness are developed. Victim mentality brings the characteristics into full view and is seen in emotional pain carriers.

Acting Out

Acting out is simply going through with the plan believed to provide an escape. Even though it offers only temporary results, the cycle continues, because what is happening within is not resolved. Sometimes an individual's pain events are such that multiple acts are attempted to bring temporary peace. If blocked, another backup plan or a new attempt will take place until the escape has been successful. If an individual does not find rest from life's pain, they may decide to quit entirely and commit suicide. I noticed that the top ten escape behaviors given by Ron Wilkins (2006) were familiar, but they may be surprising for you. They are as follows.

1) Anger: Anger is an emotion, and emotions are amoral; that is, it is what we do with our emotions that is most important and determines intent (Ephesians 4:26, 31; Colossians 3:8).
2) Talking: Talking can be slander, grumbling, or complaining (Philippians 2:14; 1 Peter 4:9; Colossian 3:8); lying about situations or people (Matthew 15:19; Mark 10:19); and giving animosity toward individuals (Romans 3:13–14).
3) Sexual: Sexual behavior takes many forms whether it is viewing pornography, voyeurism or acting out in other ways (Galatians 5:19; Matthew 5:27–28).
4) Eating: Eating disorders can range from anorexia (refusal to eat) to bulimia (overeating and then forcing oneself to throw up) to gluttony (Proverbs 23:21).
5) Smoking/vaping/tobacco use (snuff, dip, chew, etc.): This escape pattern can create a habit that induces the need to act out even when there is no stress being experienced.
6) Alcohol: Likewise, alcohol is a psychotropic (affecting the brain) that increases depression and depressive states. Though an individual looks for escape by drinking, it is illusive.
7) Drugs (legal or illegal): Drugs can alter reality and can induce euphoric states. They can also affect the performance of the brain and create a cycle of addiction that takes on a life of its own.
8) Stealing: Stealing fulfills both the desire to possess and have the power to take. At a survival level, the need for food when it is not being provided or the fear of not having enough food can prompt stealing as well.

9) Gambling: There is excitement and physical allurement with lights, sounds, and the possibility to win and be a known as a winner. It can produce a feeling of being alive.
10) Work: With this escape pattern, there are benefits like getting paid overtime or being known as the workplace champion. After all, it feels good to be recognized by others, and it feels good to be productive.

Shame, Guilt, and Fear

Shame, guilt, and fear are interesting parts of this cycle because it is not always as straightforward that some may believe. I recognize there is legitimate shame about not being able to stop, guilt about not being a strong enough person, or fear that they will be caught. But I also see another side, in that there may also be a lot of false shame, guilt, and fear that is occurring. How can an individual tell the difference when a life pattern has been set?

In a mall or any major office building, there is usually a directory or map to indicate, "You are here." First, one must recognize where they are to be able to walk fully in truth, instead of being caught up within historic falsehoods that have been allowed to flourish. But an individual can only do what they know. For example, verbal abuse while growing up may leave an individual with the belief of not having any value or hearing, "I wish you were never born." Second, an individual's maladaptive self-concepts or false ideas formed for survival in their life are strongholds that need to be identified. Finally, helping an individual to that safe zone where they can have confidence to put all their faith, hope, and trust in God is challenging but not impossible.

Resolving to Stop

Resolving to stop is the desire to no longer live in the same pattern of existence. Unfortunately, the desire to stop by one's own will is not enough. Promises are made, and items used to act out are disposed of or destroyed. It is not the first time, though, and many family members are reluctant to believe change is even possible after a while. This situation increases the shame, guilt, and fear within individuals. Repentance is the ability to choose to stop going in one direction, but for some reason, relapse happens again.

Attempt to Act Normal

Normalization is attempted, but the underlying causation to the pattern has never been addressed. Substitution or switching from one escape behavior may occur, but it is still an escape behavior. The reality is that we all have our escape behaviors just like any other addict; it is simply that some addictions are more socially acceptable or legal than others. When examining the substitution principle, if an individual comes off cigarettes and begins using chewing tobacco, snuff, or even vapes, it is easy to recognize. It produces a kind of self-will to hold on, leading to white-knuckle living, waiting for the inevitable to take place. Then the next pain event occurs, leading to the next roundabout.

Sound familiar? It may be illusive, but examine your own interactions in life, and you may discover the pain cycle may be all too familiar. But the good news is there is help and hope.

— 4 —

The Greater Hope

While I was teaching the SFT Awareness program and strengthening its structure by using a more scriptural approach and application, this question came to my mind: "If the pain cycle is readily identified by people in the world about where they are at, does God's Word say anything about a healing process in the Scripture?" The answer is yes! From many years through my own personal and educational biblical studies, I knew of the passage in 2 Peter 1:8–11 (ESV) that explained an action process that promises the following:

> For if these qualities are yours and are increasing, they keep you from being ineffective or unfruitful in the knowledge of our Lord Jesus Christ. For whoever lacks these qualities is so nearsighted that he is blind, having forgotten that he was cleansed from his former sins. Therefore, brothers, be all the more diligent to make your calling and election sure, for if you practice these qualities you will never fall. For in this way there will be richly provided for you an entrance into the eternal kingdom of our Lord and Savior Jesus Christ.

Peter's message is compelling because of the great promises being made. I will restate what they are: (1) They keep you from being ineffective or unfruitful in the knowledge of our Lord Jesus Christ. (2) If you practice these qualities, you will never fall. (3) There will be richly provided for you an entrance into the eternal kingdom of our Lord and Savior Jesus Christ.

Using the behavioral cycle (Wilkins, 2006) as an example, I applied the pattern shown in 2 Peter 1:5–7, and God's healing process was developed (see Fig. 2).

Figure 2. God's healing process theory

As one obeys the Gospel, they are added to the Church by God (Acts 2:38–41, 47) and enter God's grace, which is in Christ Jesus (Ephesians 2:8; 2 Timothy 2:1, 10). People need to hear and know about Jesus and the Gospel (Romans 1:16–17; 1 Corinthians 15:1–4; 2 Thessalonians 1:8–10) before they can make an individual choice to believe or not to believe in Jesus. By becoming convinced about Christ, they turn away or repent (Acts 17:30), and they stop themselves from continuing to do wrong (Romans 6:1–2). By beginning and continuing their confession of faith in Him before others (Matthew 10:32–33), and by being united with Him in baptism, they enter into God's grace (Romans 6:3–14; Acts 2:38, 41, 47; 1 Peter 3:21–22; Colossians 1:5–6; 2:8–14). It is not an exclusive event like checking a box because it requires an individual to continue to be faithful till death (Revelation 2:10).

Upon looking at God's healing process, there are certain aspects to consider. Peter begins explaining in 2 Peter 1:3–4 that God's power through Christ offers us the divine connection to free us from the allurement of the sinful desires (lust) that have corrupted the world. I believe Peter's approach is one of a stepped process with an accumulative, simultaneous progression because there are stressed elements of each part being built upon the next within a continual spiritual growth. This is a holistic concept in that change happens from within as we submit ourselves to the will of God. The idea in 2 Peter 1:9 also shows if we have a lack of these qualities, we are being nearsighted and blind. Each part of the process described is necessary for the next to take place. With further work using and applying GHP principles within my own life, I also began helping other individuals who were seeking help. There was an ongoing process that needed to be experienced in recognizing the developmental principles being discovered.

WHAT IS THE MIND?

If asked, "Where is your mind located?" some would point to the head, where the brain is held. The reality is that your mind is your whole being, which extends throughout the body to the brain itself and from the brain to the body. As the psalmist David wrote, "I am fearfully and wonderfully made" (Psalm 139:14 ESV). The battle within the mind is not limited to the frontal cortex region. The work and application to understand how the brain operates continues. By developing a foundation and formational understanding of how the brain works, we can begin to grasp the challenges that occur when an individual undergoes a trauma event. Trauma can also affect the procedural development of the brain, which can leave an individual trapped in a survival mode. Victim mentality also takes place, and the basic concept of the behavioral cycle is brought into a better understanding. So let's look at the reason why.

In general, there are three different general segments of the brain that filter and store life experiences. The base brain, which some secular scientists refer to as the reptilian brain (neocortex), stores body memories, or what is felt physically during an event. The mammalian brain (limbic system) is the emotional storage region, which is the emotional experience of the event. The frontal cortex is the region that is related to logic, reason, and creativity. Thanks to spectrograph devices, imaging can now take place within different regions of the brain, which allows a better understanding of what is happening to an individual. What was noticed? The frontal cortex, which is the logical processing section, is shut down (along with other body functions) during a traumatic event. Trying to outthink the deeper parts of the brain creates problems and can lead an individual into living a lie through denial of their life experience. An example of this is when well-meaning people make statements like, "You shouldn't feel this way." Instead of integrating a traumatic experience, it isolates the experience, labeling it as being dangerous. Emotions and feelings are then left isolated and labeled as bad, which creates a divided self.

To fill in the blanks left when the cognitive reasoning comes back online, false memories can be created to try to help an individual rationalize their experience. These faulty thinking patterns of deception exist to help move forward in life, which may inadvertently also create more stress and depression. Basically, you cannot outthink your brain. I have seen individuals argue that everyone is accountable for their decision and actions, however the driving force that exists to live and survive another day will overrule logic.

When comparing the GHP process with the Pain Event Cycle, notice the overlapping shifts:

- The grace event takes the place of the pain event. There it begins and continues the on-growing process we have in Christ (Colossians 1:3–6).
- Faith takes the place of rumination. We walk by faith, not by sight (2 Corinthians 5:7 ESV; Romans 10:17; Hebrews 11:1, 6).
- Virtue (good works) takes the place of depression (Philippians 4:8).
- Knowledge takes the place of stress (Colossians 2:2–8; Philippians 4:6; Matthew 7:11; Luke 11:13).
- Self-control takes the place of the decision to escape. Self-control is also based on faith (1 Corinthians 10:13). The decision to fix ourselves (having a quick fix to feeling good) inhibits the Spirit working in us to produce the long-term healing God desires for us to have. We must have more faith in Him and the work He is perfecting in us (Philippians 1:4; 2:13). As this growth takes place in our life, we mature and are no longer shaken about (Ephesians 4:13; Hebrews 5:1–11).
- Steadfastness (patience) takes the place of a plan to escape. The old patterns are replaced by a new way of life (Matthew 6:33;

Ephesians 2:13; Colossians 2:13–14; Romans 6). The old patterns and plans (strongholds) must be replaced (Matthew 12:43–45; Matthew 9:7; Mark 2:2; Luke 5:37–38; Luke 11:24–26).
- Godliness takes the place of acting out. Godliness is when we begin to see the world in the way God sees it, which moves us to brotherly kindness. Our "acting out" step is changed from acting out of selfish desires or survival behaviors into a positive response to our and others' needs through Christ (Philippians 2:4, 21). We become motivated through compassion, which becomes having brotherly affection (kindness) in the active expression of the love of God.
- Likewise, because of our growth, we have no false shame, guilt, or fear. We live in a condition of peace, being unashamed and assured of whom we are in Christ Jesus (Romans 8:1; 2 Timothy 1:7).
- Godliness leads to brotherly affection (kindness), which takes the "resolving to stop" step because there is nothing to hide, and we recognize other people with grace and without condemnation. We become enabled to act with the compassion of Christ in serving one another (Hebrews 6:10–12).
- Love takes the attempt to act normal position. It is the resultant effect of all previous steps mentioned in the development (1 Corinthians 13; 1 John 4:18).

Therefore, grace begets grace. We become an extension of God's grace as Christ works through us to make an effectual difference in others (Ephesians 2:1–10). The damaged areas of human endeavor are also answered through God's Word (see Fig. 4). As we are doing God's Word (James 1:22), healing can take place.

THE COMMANDMENTS OF CHRIST

Have you ever noticed that the commands Christ and the Holy Spirit, through the scriptures, gave for us to do were external of oneself (Matthew 25:35–46)? Through the Holy Spirit, James wrote about the necessity of having an active faith to produce understanding that helps us develop (James 1:22–27; 1 Peter 1:3–9). The opposite would be following the world's advice of being self-serving and relying on oneself to produce joy. An example would be an open hand versus a closed fist (see Fig. 3).

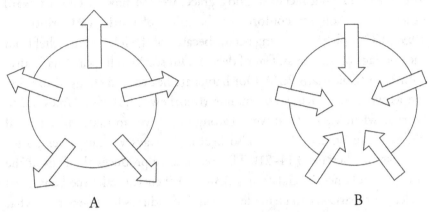

Figure 3. Open hand (A) and closed fist (B) examples

Draw a circle on the palm of your hand; that circle represents you. Notice how, by doing Christ's commands, we are positioned outside (open hand) of ourselves. God's power works through us as we obey what Jesus said to do to heal us in ways we never can. Likewise, when we act out of selfish ambition, we become closed off, and the power of God is being cut off from being effective. In the open position (A), Christ's light shines forth, and in the closed position (B), darkness prevails. In another example, the living waters either flow forth (A) or are closed off (B) from being effective in God's healing process for ourselves and others; grace begets grace (John 13:15; Luke 16:13; John 12:26).

When people look at the pain cycle, they recognize the pattern of addictive cycles they have had in their life. Likewise, by looking at God's healing process (see Fig. 4), they can recognize where they are at in relation to God's process to determine where and what should be happening. This diagram been enlightening for the Christians I have shown it to, and it presented them with a plan of action in strengthening their faith and closer walk with God. Contrasting God's healing process to the behavior cycle has similarities to John's examination between darkness and the light (1 John 1:5–10).

What similarities are seen? The pain events that occur cause pain events within us and to others. Likewise, the grace event causes the extension of grace within us and to others. Pain begets pain, and likewise, grace begets grace. Having been forgiven, we can now forgive with appropriate forgiveness. Having received God's grace, we can now extend it toward others. Our thoughts conform to the mind of Christ (2 Corinthians 10:3–5). Our physical healing occurs because of the release and relief from the bondage of sin (stress, fear of death). Our spiritual lives are made alive with Him (Colossians 2:13). Our habits are healed and changed to bring life as we obey Christ's commands (Matthew 25:31–40; James 1:27), because when we let God work through our lives to make an effectual difference in others, He can also heal us in ways we can never do for ourselves (Ephesians 3:14–21). This repentance produces the fruit of the Spirit as explained in Galatians 5:13–26. When you take the behavioral cycle, a comparison can be made with an individual's life to examine what is being produced in it. Take a moment and notice how the exhortations made in 1 John 1:4–10 and 1 John 2:1–6 are more readily identified and able to be accomplished.

Wilkins (2006) noted that pain events mostly stem from the damage or unmet needs included in universal human endeavor. This idea is also reflected in the principles of Maslow's hierarchy of needs. Unmet needs may or may not have trauma associated with them. However, the reactance mode or survival mode is very similar. Remember, trauma is subjective to the individual who experiences it; likewise, pain events are also subjective. I have noticed people try to ignore trauma and pain events, but the undercurrent still exists and drives individuals in ways to live in survival mode. When we decide to enter into God's healing process, areas of human endeavor begin to also be healed and answered.

Figure 4. God's healing process (Copeland 2011).

When Jesus said, "If you abide in my word, you are truly my disciples, and you will know the truth, and the truth will set you free" (John 8:31–32 ESV), please note that this did not mean the truth will make you feel "happy." If anything, it reinforces what James recognized in his life (James 1:2–3): he would rejoice in various trials and tribulations because he recognized that his faith was being refined by God. Instead of being in a state of darkness, surviving and playing the part of a victim, we are able to be transformed: we become enlightened, thriving, and victorious over life's circumstances.

THE AREAS OF HUMAN ENDEAVOR

By looking at the areas of human endeavor through the lens of the scripture, we begin to see a pattern that allows for healing to begin.

Survival

"I am the door. If anyone enters by me, he will be saved and will go in and out and find pasture" (John 10:9 ESV). One of the best aspects to realize is that the transformational process we can achieve through Christ moves us beyond living in a survival mode. One of the biggest issues that can occur is when individuals learn to survive by becoming victims of life and being overcome by circumstances.

Dr. Daniel Amen (2008) wrote in *Healing the Hardware of the Soul* that the brain has over one quadrillion synaptic points, which equates to more stars than can be counted in the sky. Simply stated, we have the capacity for genius, but most people have learned only to be genius at survival! Through God's healing process, we are called to no longer be slaves to sin, but we are becoming His workmanship of righteousness. God's righteousness is being made manifest and complete through Christ as we allow God's access in our lives.

> So that, as sin reigned in death, grace also might reign through righteousness leading to eternal life through Jesus Christ our Lord. (Romans 5:21 ESV)

> And be found in him, not having a righteousness of my own that comes from the law, but that which comes through faith in Christ, the righteousness from God that depends on faith. (Philippians 3:9 ESV)

Acceptance

We all have an inborn need for connection and attachment. Going back to Genesis 2:18, we find the earliest recognition that it is not good to be alone. If we do not feel accepted, some may conform their behavior to the immediate social narrative or peer group, even when it is destructive. God gives us unconditional acceptance with where we are, with the expected condition of not remaining in that separated state. For example, if a helicopter came to rescue you during a flood from the roof of your house, you cannot remain on the roof and be saved from the flood.

> For God so loved the world, that he gave his only Son, that whoever believes in him should not perish but have eternal life. (John 3:16 ESV)

> For if their rejection means the reconciliation of the world, what will their acceptance mean but life from the dead? (Romans 11:15 ESV)

Pleasure

Pleasure is more than just feeling good. It is a state of being that allows joy, contentment, and peace to be experienced in our life. Our faith in action is formed from His divine purpose; we enter that greater state of grace existence, which gives resolve to our willingness to be spiritually transformed. The need of pleasure is answered by gaining access and actively participating in what is truly good and everlasting.

> Instead, seek his kingdom, and these things will be added to you. Fear not, little flock, for it is your Father's good pleasure to give you the kingdom. (Luke 12:31–32 ESV)

> Therefore, my beloved, as you have always obeyed, so now, not only as in my presence but much more in my absence, work out your own salvation with fear and trembling, for it is God who works in you, both to will and to work for his good pleasure. (Philippians 2:12–13 ESV)

Power

What is your idea of power? Where does it come from? What power controls you? There are two primary powers in life. One is based on fear, and the other is based on love. The outcome of life depends on which power source you are plugging into: fear leading to death, or love leading to life. Living in survival mode without hope is powered by fear. The power transition from fear to love comes from leaving survival mode with hope. Remember that power within itself is nothing and meaningless without love (1 Corinthians 13). The area of human endeavor of power is answered by realizing and realigning oneself with God through Christ daily.

> For God gave us a spirit not of fear but of power and love and self-control. (2 Timothy 1:7 ESV)

> Now to him who is able to do far more abundantly than all that we ask or think, according to the power at work within us, to Him be the glory in the church. (Ephesians 3:20–21 ESV)

Freedom

Freedom and slave mentality are a reality. Those living in fear and reacting in life have a conditioned existence of a type of slave mentality. There are no exclusive race or gender types needed to qualify someone to have slave mentality. Just play the victim role. What role are you playing in life? The truth is many have been programmed and conditioned for having a slave mentality. Notice that in Exodus, four hundred years of slavery conditioned Israel into wanting to turn back to Egypt even after being witness to God's miraculous power to free them. To be clear, this is about an individual's or even a culture's thought process leading to imprisonment out of fear. Freedom mentality is empowered and driven by love. When we stop living in falsehoods created by thinking errors and enter new thought patterns of truth, spiritual transformation is accessed. The pattern of being a slave to sin leading to death is now broken through Christ.

> For the law of the Spirit of life has set you free in Christ Jesus from the law of sin and death. (Romans 8:2 ESV)

> For you were called to freedom, brothers. Only do not use your freedom as an opportunity for the flesh, but through love serve one another. For the whole law is fulfilled in one word: 'You shall love your neighbor as yourself.'" (Galatians 5:13 ESV)

I have heard it explained by different popular Christian theologians that there is an empty void where the heart is, and it needs to be filled with the love of Christ. Sadly, these types of oversimplifications of what is "felt to be true" may be leaving individuals feeling further rejection, self-repulsion, and even alienation from Christ. I have met several individuals who have had these experiences and lived in those types of situations of guilt and shame. GHP has helped these individuals gain new insight and realization to what has happened. The education of how the mind works helps individuals know they are not going crazy! It also helps work within that design setting to learn new approaches through empowerment that He provides.

The challenge is the brain has, by design, set up procedures to survive. Individuals are attempting to escape that setup, but it seems inescapable as evidenced by the pain event cycle. The genius of survival from deeper regions of the brain, from the limbic system and base brain, overpowers and trumps logic and cognitive functioning.

For some, there is an idea that Jesus can take care of all problems apart from our doing anything or interacting with living life. Though it sounds good, it also negates God's work being accomplished within us. If we refuse God's power working through us, we rely upon our own strength and reasoning. It is not a power of our own, not of self-righteousness, nor is it a work accomplished by our own will (Ephesians 3:11–21). If we are His ambassadors, then we represent Him when and as we meet others every day. Can we sit at home and pray only that Jesus takes care of what He has given us to accomplish through His commission (co-mission) with us (John 17)?

For example, if a car was broken down, would we simply wash the outside of it to make it work again? Would we give it a new paint job and put in a new air freshener? Of course not! I have found that by understanding the nature and genius of God's design, individuals can begin to grow and realize what is happening inside of them by design.

— 5 —

Grow Beyond the Known

You can't give what you don't have.

Over the years, I have come to appreciate the working of God as being an important part of and in my life. Even though I may not have always understood the direction that He was leading, or being in places with circumstances that were less than desired, it ultimately worked for good. For many people who struggle with control issues, recognizing that there is greater work being accomplished without understanding is challenging. The idea of letting go and letting God is a matter of trust and faith that needs to be developed. In God's healing process, there is a maturation process that, when applied, develops being able to put more of an individual's faith, hope, and trust in Him. As I matured and grew in many ways in Christ, I saw that walking by faith means trusting God regardless of circumstances. Losing personal expectations and staying curious allows a smoother transformational process to be revealed. Faith in action gains practical experience and bolsters confidence in relational growing with God through Christ and the Holy Spirit.

Historically, I have been through many schools of thought when approaching my walk with faith and direction in life. Some were described by Dennis Horton. Horton (2009) examined three ideologies in the practice of discernment of finding God's will: the Bull's-Eye Approach, the Wisdom Approach, and the Relationship Formation Approach.

The Bull's-Eye Approach was identified as a more traditional view in which our lives have a specific meaning and purpose being revealed by God to that person as they experience life (Horton 2009). People who use this technique make decisions waiting for a feeling of peace to be given from the Holy Spirit to affirm or otherwise condemn them. Horton indicates the Bull's-Eye Approach uses prayer is like a global position satellite as an indicator of being on track with God's will or combined with being given a sign. Horton notes tendencies in finding God's perfect will for their lives include finding and prescribing decision-making processes and formulas. Some may tend to scoff at the processes and formulas being humanly biased. Schaffer (2008, 779–99) brings the very idea to illuminate human tendencies, in that

> religion produces moral codes to help individuals justify themselves, but also produces theodicies which seek to justify the actions of the gods. Since cultural institutions differentiate themselves from each other by pursuing distinct ideological goals, religion also emerges as a separate cultural institution by pursuing the goal of finding meaning in life experiences.

That being said, there can be a plausibility that an individual can act within the Bull's-Eye Approach under the cloak of seeking God's will while being self-serving.

Charles Swindoll (1996) spoke about being wary of self-deceptions and having ways of recognizing being drawn away. Swindoll gives four practical steps in identifying whether or not a person is focusing in the right direction. First is paying close attention to what you are looking at, second is giving greater consequences of sin rather than its pleasures, third is beginning each day by renewing your sense of reverence for God, and fourth is focusing fully on Christ throughout the day. Notice the formula given by Swindoll gives some insight into how to combat against the idea brought to light and proposed by Schaffer. Swindoll also gives scriptural application to support each of the ideas brought forth. One element found missing is the behavioral aspect or why a person's inner drive to find and achieve balance is activated.

Horton (2009) recognizes the Wisdom Approach, which is defined as people relying on their God-given reasoning abilities, wise counsel, with recognition of clear strengths, talents, and abilities. The two aspects Horton indicates are the Biblical Wisdom Emphasis and the Pragmatic Christian Wisdom Emphasis. Both ideas give an indication of a general will of God in a person's life rather than a specific path. The direction being sought after in the Wisdom Approach is in working within the understanding of God's general will, being Christlike in all situations in life, and being guided by the principles found in His Word. The challenge with these ideas are individuals with adverse childhood experiences (ACEs), who have left a trail of trauma and survival modes (strongholds) that have been implanted in an individual in order to survive another day. Basically, you can't build a house during an earthquake.

The Relationship Formation Approach deals with an intimate relationship with God through our formation in Christ (Horton 2009). The analogies of the shepherd and the sheep and the relationship of a loving parent with a child, emphasizes the idea of a developing the individual within the capacity of making mature responsible decisions. This idea is supported by the Bible as the work of Christ in us and the refining of our life to reflect Christ (Ephesians 3:20; Romans 8; 1 Corinthians 13:12; 1 Peter 1; 2 Peter 1:1–10). Once again, patterns of trauma can interfere with attachment to an unfamiliar shepherd and even God.

PAST AND PRESENT INFLUENCES

For myself, I recognize having been, at various stages, guided by influences from my parents and congregational experiences, and I have sought spiritual enlightenment through other sources, which led me back to God's purpose for our lives. At different stages of my life, I tried the Bull's-Eye Approach, and I sought after God's will using the Wisdom Approach as well. I believe each had a part in helping me to grow into being more spiritually aware of God's true calling of each of us beyond our own self-interests.

While growing up in the church, I had been working through my life with the Wisdom Approach, but it lacked the application I saw in the scripture among people professing Christ. I saw they tended to be self-centered, and the Wisdom Approach produced self-righteousness people with those I knew. As an adolescent, I experienced some of the darkest times of my life while trying to find meaning in my life by helping

God through other spiritualism and natural ways. I soon discovered the true power of God is incomparable to anything I could ever try to do otherwise. As my journey in life continued, I worked through the Bull's-Eye Approach, looking for God's will in my life (as I saw with examples of those around me). Still, I found my tendencies being drawn toward a self-centered relationship with God. My foundation of faith was being built on the survival mode of existence, which left me reacting to situations instead of responding in love.

While in the military, I worked through a combined effort of the Bull's-Eye and Wisdom Approaches, and I could not make them align with a walk with Christ the way I read the early Christians had. During deployments (including supporting combat missions deployed around the world), I continued the habits of searching God's Word with fasting and prayer. I had learned and discovered that when I served God, my life was better, so I dug deeper (Hebrews 11:6). I attempted to take my relationship with God more seriously and continued to seek after His will for my life.

During a remote tour in Korea, I diligently studied and prayed for a greater understanding, and it was given to me. It allowed for a catalyst of growth in my personal life that I also found others were looking for and missing in their lives. I found it wasn't about doing what God wanted you (your will) to do, but you letting God work through you (God's will) to make an effectual difference in other people's lives. The understanding of godliness comes into focus when we apply our faith in action. Godliness is being able to understand God's vision of the world through Christ. Our enemy is not our enemy but is an individual without understanding or connection to God's love (Romans 12:15–21). Through our ongrowing faith, we are ambassadors (2 Corinthians 5:20).

Have you ever noticed all the commands Christ gave in Scripture are external from oneself? Some that come to mind are feeding those who are hungry, clothing those who are naked, visiting orphans and widows, and visiting those who are in prison. I discovered that when we obey Christ's commands, God can work through us to make a difference in other people's lives. In addition, as that takes place, He can heal us in ways we never could or can imagine. This explains James writing, "Be ye doers of the Word, not hearers only thus deceiving yourselves" (James 1:22 ESV).

Have you ever wondered, "Am I doing God's will in my life?" I believe

GHP can be used as a tool to refocus and realign individuals as needed. Personally, I have found GHP useful to change old habits and place better priorities on spiritual growth. First, recognize the importance of doing God's will in your life. Second, pray and ask God for clarification of your definition or understanding of what is doing God's will. This will help establish where you are coming from philosophically. One's personal understanding of God's Will reflects which approach may have been taken or learned from the past.

I began by using the Wisdom Approach of understanding God's will. I addressed any issues of being afraid and asked, "What am I afraid of?" In many cases, there is no need to be afraid, but we may have learned to be afraid from damaged human endeavors. Issues like what career to choose are not dealing with salvation issues, as mentioned in Philippians 2:12, but they can be brought into light of 2 Timothy 1:7 (ESV): "For God gave us a spirit not of fear but of power and love and self-control."

Have an insightful consideration to the attributes and talents that God has given. This may be instrumental in helping discover what God has enabled you to accomplish. Having testing done to identify interests and personality types, such as the Arno Profile System, can also help define potential direction. Consider information about family history and have a genogram done. Genograms are a great way of placing family history and relative dynamics that have influenced family directions and interaction.

Don't be afraid to explore decisions made thus far in life; recognize personal, parental, and relationship decisions that are made every day and that are made by faith because we have an ongoing relationship with God. For instance, God did not choose the clothes you decided to wear today or the food you put in your mouth. These everyday decisions He entrusted individuals to make for themselves. Gain personal understanding and overcome potential thinking errors coming from the past. Some of these issues are also explained by John Ortberg in his book *God Is Closer Than You Think*. Ortberg (2005) points out that each person experiences God differently because we are made differently. Ortberg suggests that our individual uniqueness should be understood instead of attempting general social experiments that cannot help us reach and understand God in our life. In addition, there is a need to recognize trauma's influence, which inhibits and interferes with who God created us to be because it is based on fear.

While I may not always recognize my personal position with God's will working in my life, I have come to understand it is a dynamic flow of existence. I may not get to be where I think I want, but I have learned to always trust God, because what He has in mind is much greater than what I ever expected. GHP is ultimately learning how to be in attunement with God's grace, be aligned, be at peace, and become that extension to others. The universal principle I recognized is, "You can't give what you don't have." Basically, if you don't have grace, you can't give grace; if you don't faith, you can't give faith; if you don't have love, you can't give love; if you don't have Jesus, you can't give Jesus. If you took inventory today, what do you have spiritually that you can give to others? What about forgiveness?

— 6 —

Coming Out of the Darkness

It is the most difficult, easy thing to do!

The idea of darkness is akin to ignorance. However, it is written that "God once winked at this ignorance, but now holds everyone accountable" (Acts 17:30–31 ESV). Godliness is achieved when we humble ourselves to the realization that (1) it has never been about us, (2) we cannot fix ourselves, and (3) acceptance of God's grace comes first before we can become His extension of grace to someone else. God's ultimate grace is based in the gospel of Christ.

As I went through the SFT process, I was able to begin to actually "take every thought captive" (2 Corinthians 10:5–7 ESV). As my deception in my life was being removed, I began to read passages of scripture with greater accuracy. The dynamics of interpersonal relationships in the scripture became more evident and applicable in my own life. I began teaching and showing others as well and noted that when it came to showing people the behavior cycle (pain cycle) for the first time, they nearly always said, "That's my life." I even remember saying that to Gary Washer when I was trained in the program myself. Aspects of escape patterns also revealed a pattern in my own life to which I was not proud of; I learned how human I really am. To face oneself in the reality of truth is what the Scripture talks about being able to do in James 1:25 (ESV), "looking into the perfect law, the law of liberty." It sounds easy enough, right? But if we have learned to lie to ourselves, even when we focus in the "perfect law of liberty" (God's Word), we will never come to the correct knowledge or understanding. We will misapply and religiously hold to that which is false without ever knowing the truth; I would also call this existing in a stronghold. I discovered I was going to die while being in a lie and would have never known it. Does this sound familiar? Jesus tells us plainly, "Not everyone who says to me, 'Lord, Lord,' will enter the kingdom of heaven, but the one who does the will of my Father who is in heaven" (Matthew 7:21–23 ESV). I had read that passage many times before believing it to be true—but without applying to myself because I was "okay." Yet a closer look at this passage reveals that they felt confident in their relationship with God. After all, they prophesied, cast out demons, and had many "mighty works" in His name, and they did not make it to heaven. Instead, they heard something shocking: "Depart from me, I never knew you, you workers of iniquity." Perhaps you are where I was at one time, feeling comfortable and assured because of a ministerial job position or given title, with a known work performance and reputation. After all, we are known by our fruit that is being produced in our lives. The only difference between the word *lives* and the word *lies* is the letter *v*. *V* can stand for either victim or victory. If we only survive and remain in victim mode, there is no victory. If we make claim to our own way in self-righteousness apart from God, we are living in vain.

If our victory is not in Jesus Christ, then our lives truly are lies. How can we worship God in Spirit and in truth while walking in darkness? The process of GHP theory begins with the recognition from an individual's understanding of their current state of being. That is, you are either walking in either darkness or light.

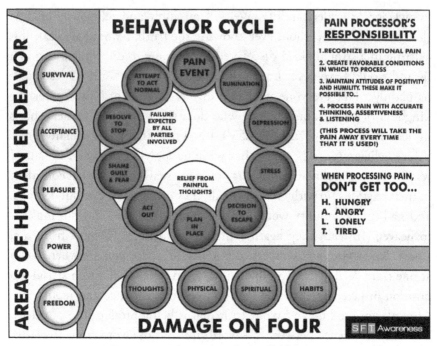

Figure 5. Behavior Cycle (Wilkins 2006)

Using the behavioral cycle that Ron Wilkins described enables individuals to relate and recognize their own experiences of life to what would be darkness. By comparing both diagrams together, using God's healing process (see Fig. 6), it may be possible to help individuals gain insight and accurately recognize where they exist for themselves. Many individuals believe that they are "okay." Unless an individual examines themselves in the fullness of God's truth, what will be the result? Second Corinthians 13:5 (ESV) says, "Examine yourselves, to see whether you are in the faith. Test yourselves. Or do you not realize this about yourselves, that Jesus Christ is in you?—unless indeed you fail to meet the test!" So, are you walking in darkness or the light?

GOD'S HEALING PROCESS

Figure 6. God's Healing Process (Copeland, 2011)

As we follow the circle, we find that the grace event takes the place of the pain event. There it begins and continues the ongrowing process we have in Christ (Colossians 1:3–6). By looking at both diagrams, I realized the transformational state and refinement process that is taking place. It is God's healing process being accomplished. First, an individual must have a willingness to be refined or healed. It is a transitional stage coming out of being a pain carrier and becoming a pain processor. Now there is a choice that individuals face: whether to continue to live in the strongholds that they have been converted to or may have built in life. The verdict is it is time to vacate those strongholds so they can be destroyed. What's in your stronghold?

While looking at diagrams and working with individuals, I also noticed the pattern that Paul described in Galatians 5:16–26. Ready? By looking at Figure 7, we may notice that we can recognize this pattern of the "works of the flesh" that Paul describes in Galatians 5:19 is happening within individuals. Individuals recognize they are living in the pain cycle despite having been Christians for decades. They believe they are "okay." What does this mean? Looking at Figure 8, we may more accurately see the conflict. It is reminiscent of Jesus's words about the Pharisees being "whitewashed tombs but inside is rotting corpses" (Matthew 23:27).

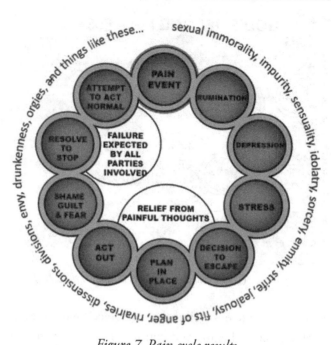

Figure 7. Pain cycle results

Figure 8. Whitewashed tombs

Perhaps some of the biggest strongholds people have are lined with gold and precious gems. Some have steeples pointing toward heaven with large columns out front. Maybe it is a legalistic stance in an understanding of scripture, or intolerance of other people's views based on a narrow band of acceptable truth. Many may have learned ways and have become confused, believing the idea of being on the straight and narrow. In reality, it may be a self-righteous stance in order to remain confident and comfortable. You can recognize Jesus's conversation with the rich young man in identifying what strongholds he had to face (Matthew 19:16–26). The justification of goodness or righteousness shown through material possessions is empty. Could these strongholds be the cause of pain events? Could strongholds created be continuing pain events?

By looking more into the concepts in God's healing process, we can see principles and recognize the light of the truth (see Fig. 9). Notice that because we are His workmanship of righteousness, it is possible to be saved only with God. Life being lived in Christ that is being spiritually transformed conflicts with works of the flesh (see Fig. 10). Notice that Figure 7 (the pain cycle results) and Figure 9 (where the fruit of Spirit is naturally manifested) make sense. Figure 8 (with the whitewashed tombs) rings true with living in a state of hypocrisy. Figure 10 is where spiritual living denies fleshy desires and the existence of both simultaneously cannot occur. Is this why sin separates us from God?

Figure 9. Fruit of Spirit naturally manifested

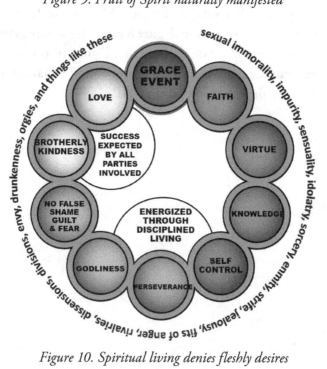

Figure 10. Spiritual living denies fleshly desires

Instead of falsehood or strongholds, a foundation of truth will enable a dwelling place to exist that cannot be shaken. For many, it is a frightening move to consider. Is it safe? To go beyond the known to the unknown takes courage, and we must have faith, knowing He will never leave or forsake us on our journey. That is why we "walk by faith and not by sight" (2 Corinthians 5:7 ESV). For myself, I recognized it was the most difficult, easy thing to do! I still help and encourage individuals in that truth that "It will be the most difficult, easy thing to do." The term *interesting* has become one of my favorites to use with life events over the past few years. It allows me to have curiosity about everything, allows an examination without judgment, and becomes an appropriate action of applied grace.

I have been blessed and given various titles with different positions of employment over the years including being a full-time youth minister. From that experience, I learned that some titles do not produce any real meaning to anything. For instance, sometimes an expansion of a job title may have a perceived benefit intended to have added value without any meaning. The greater work that God is accomplishing through us, whatever or wherever we are, is completely His. We are His workmanship of righteousness, a product of that which He is transforming and preparing us for work now and then eternity. All that I have known, no matter how incredibly wonderful or disastrously catastrophic, can be compared to the love that is in Jesus Christ. The uniqueness of His love transcends and is able to unify completely, if all are willing to truly obey and trust in Him. The search for the greater truth is revealed through diligence and His Word. Hebrews 11:6 talks about how God is a rewarder of those who diligently seek Him. But it is the application of His Word that allows deeper wisdom and spiritual transformation to take place.

Honestly, there were times that I did not diligently seek Him, especially after being told by others, "You're thinking too much." My need for others' approval and unquestioning obedience to those in charge was an inhibiting factor of the growing my faith. Then the question came: "Whom is it better to serve, man or God?" With God's healing process theory, I began to wonder whether what I learned upset those who did not want to be inconvenienced or made uncomfortable by what was being realized. I believe those who look at this book are those who are not afraid of God's truth.

One powerful and humbling moment is when all that you believe in and worked toward comes to fruition. When we walk by faith and not by sight (2 Corinthians 5:7 ESV), it does not mean a "blind" faith. God's Word is powerful; its principles are foundational to having an abundant life. What are the limits of God's ways?

Is it not any wonder that where people hate and fight change, they will also refuse to allow themselves to be spiritually transformed by God? They cut themselves off from being willing to receive anything from God. The limitations of one's belief effects everything. Paul realized this when he stated, "I can do all things through Christ who strengthens me!" (Philippians 4:13 ESV). By applying his belief and having his faith in action, God worked through him to heal him from the darkness of his past. Paul fully put all his faith, hope, and trust in Him. The question is, have you?

To know the truth, you have to study and live in truth. There have been many individuals who have professed finding the truth, but it was their understanding at that particular moment in time to which they testified. That is to say, the dynamic flow that exists is not static but ongoing. Imagine that you are floating down a river. As you are traveling, you notice new things along the way but also things that look familiar. As we come into contact through these different events, places, or people, there is a universal truth that may be noticed but also differences and variances. Greater truth will be revealed only as those who are seeking have been prepared to receive and accept. The facets of spiritual warfare are noted by Paul in 2 Corinthians 10:3–5, and the instrument for destroying strongholds is through the disciplines of prayer, meditation, servitude, and being able to be completely honest with oneself with living life. Regarding those outside ideas that have been developed, all the things that they thought they knew or understood at that snapshot in time are strongholds. These strongholds may be important for a time but need to be recognized as temporary shelters as we continue to grow in the fullness of Christ.

Jesus alluded to this in statements about wineskins (Matthew 9:17; Mark 2:22; Luke 5:37–38). The world understands that to progress in education, different steps are accomplished to assure success. There is foundational truth to build upon and grow from. However, the ultimate truth is that Jesus Christ brings cannot be built on the understanding through traditions, rules, or doctrines of humans. Fortunately, God is a rewarder of those who diligently seek Him (Hebrews 11:6). An active faith is not stagnant but is meant to be interactive like life and love. The dynamic flow that exists is constant, but the fluctuation that is experienced is based on an individual's development.

The old law was done away (Colossians 2:8–15), so that which is new may reign. That is the essential aspect of being raised up and walking in the newness of life (Romans 6:3–11) and the continued renewing of our minds in Christ (Romans 12:1–12). The old ways of our past cannot contain or survive the new ways of life, love, and hope. Everything must be made new. The question is, how do we get to that new place? Faith in name without having a faith in action is dead, however a fervent, sincere faith in action can also be destructive as well. We see this type of faith in Saul of Tarsus, who later became Paul of the New Testament. We can have a sincere faith and still be sincerely wrong. What is the difference?

Being raised in a church environment has truly been a great blessing, but it also has created challenges between what is written in God's Word and what is observed within different congregations. Even though I would like to believe that I have always been faithful, in truth I hadn't always been faithful to God. I wasn't intentionally being unfaithful to God, but I had bought into the ideas and traditions of people who had taught me. When a congregation is influenced more by the culture in which it exists rather than by God, all forms of chaos follow.

Over time, as I diligently study God's Word, it becomes more evident that though there are humans in various leadership positions, they are still fallible people who do not have all the answers. Each person has a developmental stage of growth in God, and God is still working as individuals allow. Once a person takes the stance of knowing everything, they stop growing. Some who know become filled with pride and lord over others, or they are rescuers in the drama triangle. It is an important part of humility to recognize Jesus denied being called good (Mark 10:18). Only God has all the answers, and He gives us His guidance through His Word. He has also given us the indwelling of the Holy Spirit. James 1:22 warns about becoming complacently legalistic. God's will for us is not to remain stagnant but to instead provide living water that gives life. For instance, I knew an individual who, at age ten, became a Christian and began learning how to "defend the faith" by debating God's Word, holding to a specific view of faith. He was taught how to know enough of the scriptures to validate themselves, correct error if discovered, and combat the other person's beliefs of the scriptures. He felt justified and had a sense of approval and validation with what was taught and believed right. He said, "All along the way, I have had one goal in mind: to get to heaven and take as many people as I can with me." He discovered one day after a "water cooler" debate just how badly he had missed the mark in sharing his faith. What was lacking? Telling the truth in love. When called back to work, he looked back toward the table where he had been debating. He said, "I truly remember seeing the look on his face: it was of frustration and confusion as he stared down at his Bible. At that moment, I fully realized how badly I had failed. The Bible talks about sharing the truth in love, but I was taught to go out to win one for the Lord." That realization brought personal reflection and an evaluation to what exactly was happening, leading to a new spiritual developmental stage toward greater enlightenment.

He continued, "What good is it to leave a person downtrodden, bleeding, and alone? I treated memory verses like bullets in a machine gun, and I was fully loaded." He misunderstood the relevance and application of the Bible being a sword. What is the difference? The difference between fighting with a gun is you can shoot from a distance; in sniper mode, you can do it from a great distance. When you fight with a sword, it is up close and personal. Maybe you have seen a sword fight fought by children afraid to hit each other, so they fight from a distance. Can you picture two people standing on opposite sides of a large room waving their swords in the air at each other? No one gets hit, and they both look rather silly!

If God works outside of the box, why keep trying to stay within the limitations placed by traditions of humans? Perhaps it is because that is all that is known. Perhaps most of the world's created religion is of comfort and convenience followed by power and control. Now, when a person comes to the truth, a decision can take place to either move forward in truth or stay within a comfortable belief system. It takes courage to walk in truth, to walk in the light. If one does not follow the rules of a popular church culture, what would happen?

The balance of the guilt/comfort relationship brought by religion helps people; it allows them to defer personal responsibility by being justified by works or shifting blame rather than implementing permanent transformational change. However, that idea is not what the Bible is talking about for true spiritual transformation. When reading the Bible, one may discover that Jesus did not follow the cultural flow. I illustrated this idea with a class by drawing a funnel. Inside the funnel were all different ideas and concepts flowing in multiple directions. With Jesus coming, the direction came clear because it was manifested through Him. All other ideals about directions to God, enlightenment, and spiritual transformation was contrasted and displaced with Jesus Christ providing the ultimate connection to God. What I had to realize was the foundational truth that Jesus did not come to establish another religion but to provide a direct connection back to God. If we as followers of Christ are not doing that, then what are we doing?

— 7 —

A New Beginning

Part of the background for this concept of God's healing process began with a Wednesday night adult class I was teaching called "Taking Every *thought* Captive," based on the idea in 2 Corinthians 10:3–5. I presented the foundational steps in recognizing one is an emotional pain carrier and how it interferes with spiritual growth. There are those who would confine Paul's comments to apply only with his circumstance in Corinth, battling against false gods and idols. However, the Holy Spirit, who inspired all Scripture, applies it throughout time. Even in today's culture, there are many different idols and false gods, which range from material possessions to sports teams to all lusts that are described as the fruit of the world (Galatians 5:19–21). The Searching for Truth (SFT) Awareness program helps individuals realize the plight in which they exist and gives them an opportunity to learn how to change. The overall idea of SFT Awareness is based on the theory of cognitive-behavioral therapy (CBT). Individuals can learn how to identify and choose to "take every thought captive and conform it to the mind of Christ" (2 Corinthians 10:3–5 ESV). Examining what the mind of Christ really allows individuals to learn various applications, enabling change. The problem I noticed with the SFT program was that individuals may be too anxious and unable to focus to accomplish or complete given homework assignments. Some approaches such as CBT homework, which is a part of treatment, are never accomplished by the individual because they cannot focus long enough to begin. Expecting individuals to become aligned by their own willpower will be a problem. So what about the indwelling of the Holy Spirit? Can it be helpful with individuals seeking change?

Robert Hawker, in *The Poor Man's Commentary* (1805, Romans 7:14–25), wrote that Paul recognized the two different factions at war within himself and the essential process of renewing one's mind.

> Paul saith himself in this very Chapter [Romans 7], that he was alive once, before the commandment came in this convincing light in which he saw it by regeneration. It was then only, when brought under the teachings of God the Spirit, that the commandment came, and all Paul's self-righteousness fell to the ground!

But how can an individual come to their right mind and have peace? It is no wonder that several people who seek after the Lord are disappointed when they are condemned by others for being in the state they are existing and surviving. The idea that an individual has complete control over all the circumstances in their lives is naïve and dangerous. What person has had the opportunity or power to be born into a certain demographic status, born a certain gender, or determine their parents? Yet in Christ, there is no status to be had; all are reborn new. All past sin is forgiven, and there is no longer any condemnation (Romans 8:1). The struggles we experience (trials and tribulations) are that of our lives being refined by Christ. But how do we get to that point of refinement? Because we can only do what we know, we need God's grace to allow that to be a beginning point. Each day we begin anew as we also renew our minds in Christ (Romans 12).

Noticing the amount of trauma that exists along with lack of effectiveness of traditional treatments, I began to look for more effective treatment modalities. During research, I encountered a modality called Brainspotting, founded by Dr. David Grand. During specialized training, I observed and realized, "You can't outthink your brain." That is, our cognitive processing center's operation is subject to the whole brain and greatly influenced by interaction with the limbic system and the base brain. The brain is designed for being a genius at survival; after all we are fearfully and wonderfully made (Psalm 139).

To help people better understand, I have explained it this way: trauma (pain event) is subjective to the individual's experience. We may experience that same event, but how we process and experience it may be completely different. In other words, it may be something very traumatic for me, but for you, that event may be nothing. As individuals experience something traumatic, an implicit memory occurs. A procedural memory is then formed and put in place by the brain to survive another day. Procedural memories are stored in a way that cause automatic reactions that have no ending date or time; therefore, an individual continues to be hypervigilant or anxiously waiting for the event to occur again. It is also important to note that trauma has symptoms rather than memory because of the way the brain is designed.

Theoretically, here is why: The limbic system has three basic main components called the amygdala and the sympathetic and parasympathetic systems. The limbic system is the storage area for emotional memory. When the sympathetic system starts, the activation for fight or flight begins immediately. During its power-up, it shuts down all nonessential systems for survival, which includes cognitive processing (frontal cortex) and digestive systems. During activation, it releases noradrenaline into the body, helping to numb the senses (pain) and increase respiration and heart rate. Note that when cognitive processing is shut down, the limbic system stores the emotion experienced, and the base brain stores the physical experience of events. The base brain is also used for all automatic functions and regulations within the body. Basically, when trauma occurs, it is stored in the brain as emotional and physical memories without having full cognitive awareness available.

Guess what? The brain is not the only part of the body with synaptic connections! Dr. Amen (2015, 27) has stated, "We have over hundred billion cells, with each one connected to other cells by up to ten thousand individual connections, It has been estimated that you have more connections in your brain than there are stars in the universe." We all have the potential for genius. Given the brain's capacity and memory storage process, we are all genius at survival.

Dr. Daniel Colbert, in his book *Deadly Emotions: Understanding the Mind-Body-Spirit Connection That Can Heal or Destroy You* (2003), points out that there are just as many synapses on the heart as the cerebral cortex in the brain; the stomach has twice as many, leaving some neurologists to call it the fourth brain (or gut instinct).

Bridging the gap between the processes of the natural human and the practical applications of the spirit are important. After recognizing the pattern my life was in, I discovered that most people live within this pain (behavioral) cycle. I began to question the difference between where I was and where God wanted me to be, and then I applied it to where people are and where God desires them. Instead of continuing to react to life in a survival mode and remain a victim, the need to learn to respond to life, like Jesus Christ, becomes evident. Living within the principles of God's healing process allows for the transformational process to take place.

Recognition of the connections among body, mind, and spirit help to develop and grow in a complete manner, but it is an ongoing (really an ongrowing) process. God's healing process theory is an area that continues to encompass and visualize the realization toward the completion of God's ultimate process. It is not just about removing emotional pain; it is also about being born again to a new life, a new creation, becoming like Christ. Instead of being a victim, we become victors; instead of reacting, we learn to respond, being filled with His grace. When Jesus was questioned by a Pharisee lawyer about the greatest command, His answer given (Matthew 22:36–40) is true. God's healing process gives insight to that progression and spiritual transformation intended through what Christ established through the gospel.

Figure 11 shows an idea of a developmental cycle of a maturing Christian with respect to God's workmanship of righteousness through GHP. Some have a broad brush and view the basic stages as follows: first an individual becomes convinced, then they become committed, and then they are fully converted. However, scripture gives insight into a more specific and intentional progression (2 Peter 1).

The process of transformation does not mean the denial of sin or instantly coming into the fullness of Christ. It is an ongoing process that is not forged by the will of man (Romans 9:16), but a willingness to let God complete the work that is started as one is born again (2 Timothy 3:17).

The idea presented to complete the process and progress from reacting in fear in survival mode is by becoming a pain processor (Wilkins 2006). The pain processors responsibilities are (1) recognizing emotional pain, (2) creating the favorable conditions in which to process, and (3) maintaining attitudes of positivity and humility, making it possible to (4) process pain events with proper assertiveness, thinking, and listening.

Those being healed by God recognize brokenness in themselves first, and they begin to see others in a different way by learning and growing to create favorable conditions to approach people who are in pain with positivity and humility. Approach people with a proper attitude, which involves accurate thinking, appropriate assertiveness, and attuned listening skills. Make sure the person you are meeting with is not hungry, angry, lonely, or tired (HALT; James 1:19). Meeting basic needs helps provide a platform to provide stability for the individual. So, when approaching people and extending God's grace, make sure you are not too vulnerable and fully present (Galatians 6).

This is accomplished through the indwelling of the Spirit and being empowered by God from within, having been born again (John 3:3–8; 1 Corinthians 3:1–3; 1 Peter 1:3–5, 21–25). As a newborn babe in Christ, individuals have not mastered self-control. Individuals are not instantly spiritually transformed, but it is an ongoing process being accomplished by God. A sign of spiritual growth toward maturity may be determined by whether a person only reacts to situations or whether they respond to situations. If they are reacting, that may simply mean there is more healing needing to take place from past experiences. Emotional reactivity is a subcortical process, reflecting a way of survival. How well are you doing in life's challenges?

Consider some of Jesus's examples of responding. When Jesus was at the temple driving out the money changers (John 2:14–15), notice that He took time to make a whip of cords; this gave time to consider His actions. Jesus spoke with the condemned woman caught in adultery (John 8:3–11). He took time to draw in the sand, which some have suggested may have also been an averting of His eyes from her possible nakedness. Then Jesus responded well in abating a riot and helping her move beyond the situation toward reconciliation to God. With Jesus and the woman at the well (John 4:6–11), He talked with her instead of making judgments. When Jesus was at the Mount of Olives, He healed the ear of the servant, which was cut off by Peter during His arrest (Luke 22:50–53). It is important to notice how Jesus responds to life and is not reactive.

Many times, we react out of habits that we have created to survive or learned from others' survival experiences (secondary trauma). It creates a spiritual imbalance because with trauma, we become trapped in our material existence. A lapse of self-control may be derived from a damaged belief system gone unchecked; if we no longer increase our faith, have stopped doing what God's Word says, or turned our attention away from following God's Word (specifically things Jesus said to do) by turning to other knowledge, then a relapse may occur. The lapse of self-control (not trusting in God) diminishes perseverance and does not allow godliness to be achieved. In this case, guilt is a pain that will signal the need for repentance to help produce change and healing (see Fig. 12). Remember, Godly sorrow produces repentance (2 Corinthians 7:10).

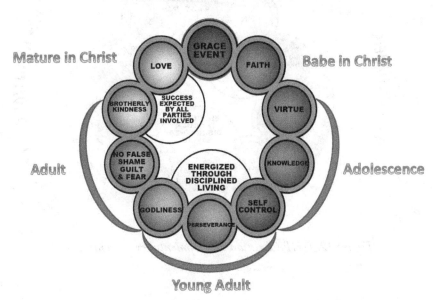

Figure 11. GHP Christian developmental cycle

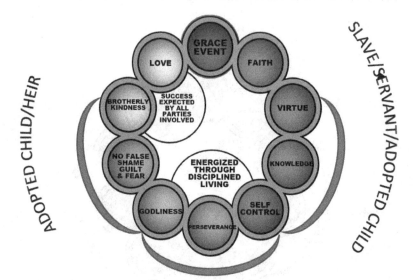

Figure 12. GHP Christian developmental cycle, continued

– 8 –
Creation Therapy and GHP Theory Dynamic

Creation therapy was developed by Richard and Phyllis Arno (1993) as a biblical approach to counseling. The approach taken is with a temperament approach; in essence, God left His thumbprint on the innermost person when made in the womb. When considering Creation therapy, temperament counseling, the pain cycle, and GHP, there are some interesting aspects of this ongoing work. There are dynamics that you may notice within yourself and the lives of individuals who are struggling through the pain cycle. The basic structures described by Creation therapy are temperament (inborn), character (learned behavior), and personality (mask).

The first structural block is temperament, and Creation therapy defines it as what God has placed within the individual while being created. The temperament structure developed is like the classical sanguine, melancholy, phlegmatic, and choleric. However, the Arnos recognized a need for a fifth temperament type and researched, developed, and included it in 1984: supine. The idea is when individuals are living outside of their created temperament, life becomes out of balance.

The second structural block of character is human and environment affected. As we are interacting with our environment and our environment with us, we learn how to survive the world in which we exist. A formula suggested by creation therapy is temperament times environment equals character.

Epigenetic studies have found that a mother's experiences and environment are encoded while individuals are being developed in the womb; this is called transgenerational memory (D'Urso and Bickner

2014). The DNA modification of cells is passed down from generation to generation in anticipation of past survival experiences and environments. It is also being noticed that even in utero, the emotional and physical experiences of the mother influence the unborn child's preparation to enter the world. When mothers already carry trauma issues, creating anxiety, the chemicals from emotions can affect the child's predisposition in order to be ready to survive. In a way, our preprogrammed perception of life's expected experiences directs us from birth out of an automatic survival or instinct mode. Once born, we then have a reinforcement of inherited survival modes that become blended with new additional survival modes.

The third building block is personality. In creation therapy (CT), personality is the idea of the self-selected mask worn based on living conditions or survival mode. The problem with wearing a mask is it is not true to who God made us be and cannot be sustained without experiencing an imbalanced life of striving. In this survival mode, personality may become a manipulation technique to get one's emotional needs met. It also can be shifted between different roles of survival leading to the Drama Triangle discussed by Dr. Stephen Karpman MD: the masks or roles people play in survival mode have three positions known as the victim, the rescuer, and the persecutor. Unfortunately, many people want without knowing what they truly need. When people remain in the drama triangle, they have a 94 percent chance of remaining stuck and unable to change. That means spiritual transformation is highly unlikely to happen and is inhibited by fear.

CT describes temperament as having three defined areas: inclusion (intellect), control (will), and affection (emotions). In basic form, when considering inclusion, control, and affection with the nature of mankind (see Fig. 13), it is interesting that each area overlaps and is in a state of pre-salvation existence or indwelling of the Holy Spirit.

Inclusion is defined by CT as social interactions and intellectual energies. Interestingly, it includes attachment from experiences and affects current associations and interactions with individuals. Poor attachment and other trauma reduce resilience and the development of the executive side of the brain (logic and reason). Trauma pain (physical, mental, or spiritual) creates fear, leaving behind fearful anticipation for more pain, which erodes feelings of safety. Reacting in fear is at the heart of the pain event cycle. In general, with trauma being present, social interaction phrases like "birds of a feather flock together" and "misery loves company" become self-fulfilling prophecies. With inclusion and the area of intelligence, it is important to remember you can only do what you know. The individual who claims to know everything unknowingly cuts themself off from limitless divine wisdom, resting in the security of their limited existence. They will not pray to ask God for wisdom because they are already convinced that they know.

Control is defined in CT as the willingness to make decisions and accept responsibility for self and/or others. In the area of control (will), notice in the pain event cycle that the pattern of reactivity is the outsourcing to control and escape pain by self-medicating or other addictive patterns. An individual who has experienced trauma or adverse conditions will be misaligned with whom God created.

This leads to an area of affection (emotion) that leads to an effort to subside emotional instability and create attachment to an individual. This may appear to become better for a time until the next pain event happens, and the pattern continues. The implanted pattern by God is encased in the shell of survival waiting to be born.

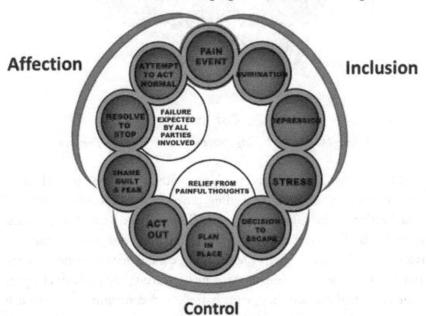

Figure 13. Pain Event Cycle within Creation Therapy

Survival modes are created through what an individual perceives to be traumatic and is by design stored in the subconscious both emotionally and physically in our brain and body. The natural survival mode is based in fear. Is this what happens within generational sin (Exodus 20:5–6; 34:7)? Is it possible that individuals are born into environments that are opposed to God, while inwardly the seed through creation has been planted by God?

Now, let's look at the areas of inclusion, control, and affection through the scope of God's healing process (Fig. 14).

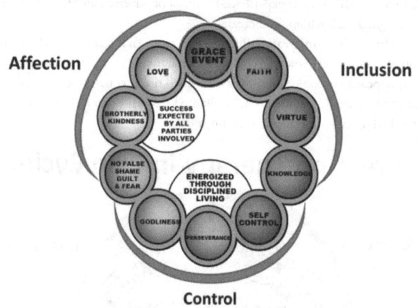

Figure 14. *God's Healing Process within Creation Therapy*

Notice that individuals working within the bounds of their temperament, through God's healing process, may best achieve the full actualization of their innermost being. Being able to break free from the strongholds of survival comes from entering God's design of salvation. It is an ongrowing acceptance of self without condemnation through Grace and obedience to the Gospel. As a new creature, an individual opens their heart without self-judgment, hatred, and condemnation, which is the trust and acceptance of God's grace. Facing the inward pain caused by survival modes allows for processing and disconnection from the past (freedom from sin) and enables a spiritual alignment and attunement to God through Christ. It continues by renewing your mind in Christ and focusing on the positive things (Philippians 4:8), enabling a continued everyday state of grace of existence with God.

Notice with GHP that the area of inclusion begins with grace. Because an individual can only do what they know, entering this new state of grace existence is necessary. God can begin to work through the individual to make an effective difference in other people's lives. That which has originated at that core begins to develop and spiritual transformation is enabled. The alignment of like-minded individuals being in association and working together in love (Hebrews 11:25; Ephesians 3:20–21) forms a unity in life and love. This reflects the prayer Jesus taught the disciples in Luke 11:2–4.

As spiritual transformation is growing, notice the area of control. It is interesting that the idea of self-control is more of an individual's willingness to place all of their faith, hope, and trust in Him (Ephesians 3:16–19). It is made possible by God's work being accomplished through us as we have our faith in action and serve others. There is a refining process happening to those historic emergency modes that were once put in place to help us survive. Perseverance through and even welcoming the times of refinement is important. James understood this and wrote, "Count it all joy, my brothers, when you meet trials of various kinds, for you know that the testing of your faith produces steadfastness. And let steadfastness have its full effect, that you may be perfect and complete, lacking in nothing" (James 1:2–4 ESV). Individuals who deny the pain from the past and refuse to be refined by God will continue to go through the pain cycle and reactive living until it is finished. When they become ready, being fed up and tired of going through the pain cycle, then healing change can be received and harmonious balance with God achieved. When an emergency mode is disconnected, greater peace is enabled in a person's life. They are no longer being tossed about in chaos. In this, continued enlightenment allows us to see things differently. An attuned vision and alignment with God allow godliness to take place within.

Notice that the area of affection is true, empowered, complete, and pure. True affection is empowered with peace that surpasses understanding because there is no false shame guilt or fear. Complete in that, as an individual continues to be refined by God, they have a developed understanding and application of God's grace in their life and the lives of others. They do not cast judgments but are able to meet individuals where they exist in that moment. They can be that extension of God's love and grace in a pure way, without malice or bitterness. "For God gave us a spirit not of fear but of power and love and self-control" (2 Timothy 1:7 ESV).

We are fearfully and wonderfully made, and upon coming into this world we are genius at survival! That which God had placed within us is awaiting a spiritual and transformational birth.

— 9 —

Dead-Ends and Detours

Going from darkness to light also implies the opposite can take place. Going from light to darkness is also possible. When well-intended individuals are going through the motions of following a belief system that takes life away rather than gives life, it creates cognitive dissonance. Cognitive dissonance is what happens when the disparity between beliefs and behaviors involves something that is central to their sense of self. It can produce feelings of being uneasy and uncomfortable from within. What is the place to find resolve? If, by turning away from the knowledge in Christ, they substitute their own system (Romans 10:1–3), they become trapped. This is really no surprise when we consider that Paul spoke about the degradation process in the first part of his letter to the Romans.

> For the wrath of God is revealed from heaven against all ungodliness and unrighteousness of men, who by their unrighteousness suppress the truth … For although they knew God, they did not honor him as God or give thanks to him, but they became futile in their thinking, and their foolish hearts were darkened. (Romans 1:18–21 ESV)

The great news is that there are options available that God provides.

There have been several generations that have had charismatic individuals who have drawn people away. This is nothing new because both Paul and Peter forewarned us that those false prophets would come and that we should not be ignorant or deceived. Many have done this in the name of God to justify their actions. Perhaps the compulsion to rely solely upon someone else's knowledge and faith to establish a relationship with God has its basis in convenience or compliance, but this goes against Peter's understanding that each person needs to be "giving all diligence" in pursuing their relationship with God (2 Peter 1:4–5 ESV). A full awakening or enlightenment needs to take place. Why not now?

The perfect spiritual disaster is when those who are unwilling to accept their personal faith responsibility are coupled with an overzealous individual who will rescue them. Each of these roles comes from unmet needs, with both individuals believing everything is going to be fine. If the one being saved feels any failure, they can rationalize feeling good by placing the blame on someone else or another person who is not helping them the way good Christians "should." Correspondingly, if the person doing the rescuing of the individual sees that person become unfaithful or failure occurs, that person becomes discarded because "they were really not that faithful anyway." Notice the strongholds, the perfect rational traps that are mental prison cells positioned on a spiritual death row. What was broken, what false belief, what hopelessness exists that people would continue down a darkened path?

For myself, I can remember times when I believed different lies because it was what I had been taught. People can be genuine, sincere, and honest and still be wrong without realizing they are doing it! It is a group thinking or mob mentality, much like the individuals who were driven into a frenzy to shout out against Jesus Christ to be crucified. How many times do we wind up being in that similar situation? It is hard to answer that question when you do not know or are perhaps unwilling to admit it. What would happen if people were honest with themselves? There is a pain that comes with truth, but it is an antiseptic that bolsters needed healing progressing toward achieving attuned enlightenment with God.

Within the world, delusions can come in many forms and are taught in many forums. Well-intended religious traditions of humans and others who are anti-Christ use destructive lies to control, ruling by fear and tyranny so people worship and honor them. This can happen even within a congregation of professed believers. Propaganda or marketing is intended to influence and manipulate to sway people's favor to move the masses to buy into an idea, whether good or bad. They will lie to others to achieve their own will without regard for the consequences to anyone else. Evil will be branded to be good, and moral-ethical values will be twisted and maligned as being evil and even intolerable. How can we escape delusions we believe to be true? If we stay closed in fear in a stronghold of survival, we will remain the prisoner of those delusions. If we have the courage to open our hearts to the greater existence of God's love to heal, the stronghold of delusion is destroyed, and then all good things become possible.

Notice how our family's emotional environment plays a part in the development of our belief system and interaction in life. The roles we learn to play to be loved, to be accepted, or sometimes to survive become our life patterns. Some of the most challenging strongholds created come from the denial of emotions because while growing up, it was explicitly forbidden to express emotions; they never learned how and don't understand how to handle them. They have never been taught anything about emotions except to avoid them at all costs. The only alternative to completely avoid emotion is to find a way to numb out and avoid, or to disassociate from life.

Providing an insight into the family history helps an individual gain a new perspective and offers new options to choose for their future. When an environment has conditioned an individual to survive, externalizing the problem from them, it will allow awareness and belief that things can change. By keeping the problem in focus, instead of shifting blame to others or self, an objective observation can be made, mistakes can be recognized, and change takes place. There are patterns of potential generational sin that may be recognized and addressed through a genogram. This tool can aid in helping an individual toward a recognition of what other influences are creating their current understanding of life. An individual may gain recognition of these patterns, establishing better boundaries as needed and choosing to move away from the drama triangle situations.

Admittedly, even if you grew up going to a church, there are things heard that became the popularly accepted idea rather than being true to God's Word. Even Paul taught and warned about traditions of people being taught as the doctrine of God. The result of these traditions is religion without substance or power. Our culture also has a hand in our development by having spoken and unspoken rules of conduct. Our genetic heritage or culture of inclusion makes us unique and can affect how we are able to cope with situations. If generational sin is evidence of how they were raised or taught to believe based on the environment they experienced, is it possible to approach individuals without condemnation? Is there evidence that our upbringing causes issues that play a part in taking the wrong direction?

We all have a choice and decision, but we also carry life experiences creating influential bias of calculated outcomes at the subcortical level. Each choice has a gain and loss associated with it. Is our decision process based on our directional bias of what we really think we want from the heart or calculated navigation from fearful expectations? What does our individual behavior and actions reveal about our vision and focus?

It can be comforting to know others share in the same struggles. Paul, in Romans 7, begins disclosing his struggles with life and the warring factions from within. Is the vulnerability we feel in becoming completely honest to ourselves echoing from the original sin in the Garden of Eden, shame? When we experience shame, we may be inwardly admitting to a fear of not being loved, a separation from a particular relationship that we feel the desperate need to have in our life. Shame also has a unique feature in that it makes it possible to be safe and survive different situations, but the limitations of shame stagnate spiritual growth. What are we looking for? Is it a relationship that gives us hope and meaning for existence?

There is an openness of love created when we can share with others while also being honest with ourselves. If we hide from relationships by covering up and denying that there is anything wrong, our state of being can readily be deceived because it has been ensnared by fear. Because most of us don't like being corrected, we tend to surround ourselves with people and ideas that make us feel comfortable. When the truth becomes an inconvenience, we can blindly stumble into error and, if not corrected, continue toward annihilation. Do not surrender or give away your power to be to anyone or anything. Inalienable rights given by God have no law against them. Do not exchange it for perishable goods or pleasures or that which is eternal for what is already passing away (Matthew 16:26).

Paul's letter to the church of Galatia asks, "Have I then become your enemy by telling you the truth?" (Galatians 4:16 ESV). However, it is interesting to note that Paul had also lived a deceived lifestyle prior to conversion. It is interesting to notice the same struggles Paul writes about can also be experienced by Christians today. Perhaps it is during the maturation process in becoming more like Christ that we begin recognizing the development of grace being accomplished from within.

Notice that condition of self-delusion that has historically existed and yet may continue to exist. Self-delusion, when it is understood, is disturbing and frightening. It can affect and shape cultural bias into actions, producing death and destruction with disregard for individual freedom. Individual freedom comes from making a path accessible by faith into that existence that is transcendent of what is known. It takes courage and honest openness to acknowledge personal shortcomings that interfere with the truth. Being able to enter that grace by faith is also being able to accept forgiveness and then be enabled to forgive.

Self-delusion inhibits enlightenment and refinement from taking place. Instead of coming to the truth and empowering others to do the same, the enforcing of desired beliefs or disbeliefs by those in power to be right must be achieved and maintained to have control. Acceptance of an imposed self-righteousness does not get anyone to heaven. Nothing may disrupt an individual's life more than having the truth revealed, but most people are satisfied with having comfort and maintaining their stronghold of lesser faith. When might or strength justifies violent actions to affront a religious belief system, then self-righteousness and human-made pride reign.

I have a Christian worldview (also called a biblical worldview), which refers to the structure of ideas and beliefs through which a Christian, group, or culture interprets the world and interacts with it. Being a fellow sojourner in this life and having made mistakes, I know I am not alone because "all have sinned and fallen short of the glory of God" (Romans 3:23 ESV). I may have been before, but I am no longer held prisoner to the weaker traditions of humans. Through Christ, you do not have to be held powerless by the traditions of humans either! When individuals have self-absorbed actions that negate the internal working of the Holy Spirit from taking place, self-delusion prevails. Maintaining appropriate humility can keep self-delusion away, but do not fall into false pride and self-abasement.

Becoming aware of being deceived at the cultural level is nothing new; in fact, it is ancient. Consider the legalism of the Pharisees in which Paul had escaped with his life. He held a strong belief in what he learned from childhood, and he even sought to enforce his belief by vanquishing this sect called the Way. What about our own cultural situations that occur? Cultural "Christianity" creates a religious base that helps people feel comfortable with where they are instead of coming to any true spiritual transformation. The reality of the kingdom of God can become twisted cultural values and levels of acceptance by the people being brought to that lesser faith. In this concept, people treat God's Word as a personal buffet and take what they like, leaving other parts untouched. One person at the buffet is eating only chocolate, another eats only vegetables, and others eat only meat. While they get what they want, they deceive themselves and never receive the full benefit from having a balanced diet that helps them be healthy. They become gluttons of self-righteousness, hearing only what they want to hear or believe. Paul talks about this idea spiritually to the church of Corinth, who was still on milk instead of moving on to the meat of the matter.

The idea here is to discuss the problem with where we are and find our way to God's will. Here are a few questions to consider: Can you come to the truth when you are still lying to yourself? Have you formally learned through this culture you are in how to systematically justify falsehoods without even knowing that it is taking place? If you discovered that you had learned to tell yourself true lies, what would your response be? What changes would need to be made?

– 10 –

An Examination of Refinement

Overcoming obstacles in life is not avoidance or denial of the situation at hand; it is about refinement. What is an obstacle? Some define an obstacle as something that gets in the way of gaining access to what is desired in life. However, there are obstacles that also protect us from harm that we may not recognize as being dangerous. Not all obstacles are physical. There are emotional obstacles that are the very strongholds that we have learned to survive in life. Because we look to escape pain and seek comfort, opportunities are limited or denied because of the limitations of existing in this survival mode. We are not made to be simply survivors of life but conquerors of darkness. We start by exiting the strongholds created and the lies that we learned to survive.

The influence of different items throughout life—people, events, food, and the like—contribute toward actions and behaviors that produce rewards. In strongholds, the search for more life and desire for connection leads individuals to seek out answers or rely upon temporary solutions that only prolong greater suffering. Instant gratification coupled with the intolerance of long-suffering leads individuals to habitual actions that can produce death in their life. The search for more life leads to less life, which then leads to more suffering and brings about a rapid, continuous, downward spiral that lies in opposition to having a satisfied or content life. Is there a solution or an end?

When considering God's healing process, there is that challenge of helping individuals exit from the stronghold of survival. It is God's refinement that is a part of healing from our past experiences that were adverse or traumatic. Entering that place for refinement has its challenges because our habits or reactive conditioning of through survival experience has been established. Refinement takes the following:

1) recognition for the need for change
2) courage
3) trust
4) honesty
5) vulnerability
6) curiosity
7) no judgment or condemnation
8) perseverance
9) continued renewal

Without the recognition that a problem exists, nothing will change, and avoidance and disassociation continue. Remember, trauma is subjective to the person who experiences it; for instance, five people can experience the same event at the same time, however, one or more may be traumatized by it while the others are not affected at all. I have noticed that in some combat veterans with complex trauma, some trauma events being processed occurred during special forces combat training. The damaged layers become a shielding for survival mode that keeps a part of the individual immobilized or frozen in the past. The shielding created for survival does not hold up and weakens over time as a person grows older.

It takes courage to move from the known survival mode into the undiscovered zone of thriving. Once an acknowledgment of a problem exists, that does not mean a person with trauma can identify it exactly. There was a reason for the brain creating the survival mode from an experienced trauma because of the experienced (perceived) danger. That protective part created stays alert for any signs of similar danger while keeping an individual from consciously noticing it. Many people avoid looking into those places because it is uncomfortable or feels unsafe. Facing the unknown takes courage, and with each courageous step, there is a gain of confidence. With that confidence, there is also an increased progression of faith. We feel safer and safer in placing more of our faith, hope, and trust in Him.

Notice that the willingness of entering refinement is also a matter of trust. With an increase in trust, an increase in safety is available; conversely, with a decrease in trust, there is a decrease in safety. Where and when does it begin? When a sense of safety beyond the stronghold exists, trust can be recognized and experienced (believed). An example of developing trust is like a parent teaching a child to swim into deep waters. The more confident and trusting a child is toward the parent, the more willing they are to enter the deeper waters. Why? Because the child believes and knows they are safe with the parent. In the same way, when we believe we are safe with God, refinement and healing become easier to acknowledge and allow (see James 1).

Honesty is a part of refinement in that a person examines themselves openly without fear, guilt, or shame. A person enters their created strongholds for safety and then stays inside with the expectation of being hurt again. The fear of re-experiencing something painful or negative can be a strong motivator to survive. When behavior is made manifest, it may help give important information about the individual's life experiences. Their behavior or reactions to life is at the subconscious level, and they may not be aware of why they are being driven. Avoidance and disassociation are survival modes producing temporary freedom from painful thoughts or memories. First John 1:7 talks about walking in the light because that is where we are needing to be transparently honest with ourselves. It is okay to realize that we are not as good as we think we are; it allows us to cast down our crowns in humility and have a greater adoration of what Christ has done for all of us.

With honesty comes the capacity for vulnerability. Vulnerability is coming out of the protective shell and being exposed to the possibility of being attacked (physically or emotionally). Most people equate vulnerability with danger because of past rejection or abandonment. There are those internalized, defensive parts that may fight against leaving the protection zone to avoid feeling pain. However, with vulnerability, there is a greater hope of healing. For example, when a child is hurt, they go to a trusted caregiver to get help because they know and believe that they will have relief from their pain. Vulnerability is not for the weakhearted; humility enables courage to access, be empowered, and gain strength through love.

Curiosity is something that can be good, but some perceive it as being bad. For example, before partaking in the tree of knowledge of good and evil, it was recorded that Adam and Eve had no shame in being naked before one another. Once the fruit was consumed, guilt, blame, shame, and fear were introduced into the world. Sin made a separation between humankind and God. Likewise, sin also makes separation and division in people, causing evil thoughts and actions to take place. Broken relationships continue to break down the ultimate connection that God wants us to have and the connection people desire by design. When people objectify one another and consider each other to be a commodity to be consumed, all forms of evil will prevail. But what does this have to do with refinement and healing? The element of curiosity allows for an individual to notice what has happened through different life events without fear and condemnation. Being curious to discover what is behind the driving force allows appropriate identification and recognition of areas for healing. Coming to the truth and applying grace where it is needed most will unravel the binds that imprison.

The step of curiosity, with applied grace, requires a nonjudgmental approach without condemnation. The truth is for most individuals who have gone through adverse life events, they reacted in a way that made the most sense at that moment. If you went back in time with the limited information you had at that moment, you would react the same way. You can only do what you know until you learn something new. In individuals with moral injuries from adverse combat conditions, there is an element of guilt for having done or been witness to something that violated their moral principles. God's healing process helps gain alignment and attunement within the fullness of God's grace to empower the individual in divine love. Beyond the pain we experience in life, greater love exists.

Perseverance is about continued endurance within the refinement process, even when painful. It is in the continued state of grace, which brings glorification of the work being accomplished. As an example, when the extraction of precious metal from ore takes place, it is put into a blast furnace and smelted. Removing the precious metal from the ore allows the metal to be further refined from impurities for practical use. When precious metals are being repurposed or recycled, there is a process where the metal is melted down to remove impurities, putting the metal in a purified state. Refinement is what most people need, but because of the fear of any pain, people avoid entering it and staying through to the end. In God's healing process, perseverance is the freedom to allow refinement to take place from within. Will you give yourself the freedom to heal?

Refinement is about not a one-time event but an ongoing process to be celebrated because of the result (1 Peter 1:6–9). The continued daily renewal allows spiritual maturity to be experienced as we are becoming more like Christ. How does that work? As different emotional reactions take place through life, therein lies an opportunity for deeper healing that may need to take place. Considering the life we live, we have learned to survive, and our true spiritual nature is hidden. We learn to perform various roles to be accepted in the hope of receiving a loving attachment, however, not all outcomes are the same. The deep-seated need to have connection or attachment is within our human design. Bad early attachment leads to increased trauma because of unmet needs. The ongoing pattern of generational issues can lead to further separation from God. Thankfully, when it is recognized, new opportunities for change can take place. Our attachment was broken from God because of sin; our attachment and connection back to God are through Christ. The stronghold layers from life's experiences from trauma may protect us from painful events, but they also keep us from being able to be fully reconciled and healed. It is much like a child who falls and is hurt. The initial pain is protected, held close to their body, and the child does not want anyone to touch it. Even when their parent tries to help, sometimes the child's fear of more pain keeps the parent from being able to help the child. The child must be able to trust the parent trying to help them so they can be helped. Without trust, healing is delayed, and more pain is experienced. In a similar way, we can do the same thing in life as adults, pulling back from God instead of coming to Him for help and healing.

In general, survival mode thrives in a drama triangle. Stephen Karpman, MD, developed the drama triangle in the 1960s. It is a representation of malfunctional social interactions, illustrated with three transitional roles: victim, rescuer, and persecutor. A person in survival mode has power struggles; each role represents common and unsuccessful reactions to conflict and shifts according to the desired outcome. Victim mentality is in contradiction with responsibility or the ability to respond. Why? Because victim mentality is reactive and comes out of survival living. There are several hundred ways of escaping the pain from broken relationships, people, and trauma pain experienced in life. These escape behaviors are what an individual will do or turn to, gaining temporary relief from painful thoughts or memories of events. Individuals may unknowingly normalize and be selective to what is good or bad based on their own life experiences or biased desires. Sadly, in our cultural existence, many are being taught how to play the role of the victim or learned helplessness. Victims blame and accuse others for having failed without recognizing the power of choice to direct different outcomes in life. Fortunately, greater hope is found by being aware and facing those fears that formed the strongholds in the first place.

Escape behaviors are evading maneuvers, which means they are temporary without relief. That means whatever past or recent events that need to be addressed can be an issue. This refinement is something that allows the past to become the historic past, instead of being held as a fearful expectation of a nonexistent present danger. If we remain either immobilized or hypervigilant by a ghost from the past, there is no end to anxiety, which wears down resilience and keeps us captive by fear leading to death.

In life, we are either reacting in fear or responding in love. The instant reaction from fear is based in survival mode, where responding in love is enabling the ability to thrive. Reacting in fear gives an indication of living in a stronghold existence. Strongholds are great for surviving, but they are not made for living life because of the limitations created. In general, a person can only do what they know, so in a stronghold, they limit their experiences to past events that they need to avoid, staying alive and not being hurt. To feel normal, they may create chaos for a familiar environment that they know and can control. The limitations of this existence guarantee the same results. Even when a person no longer feels anxious, the lack of anxiety is unfamiliar and queued as being unsafe or dangerous. The stronghold created to feel safe becomes a prison and eventually death. Where strongholds close off, limiting our visibility and distorting the perception of the world around us, in contrast, the refinement process opens and heals previously damaged areas while giving a restoration of who we were originally intended to be.

I offer an image that may represent the best conceptualization for GHP theory and its working within therapy (Fig. 15).

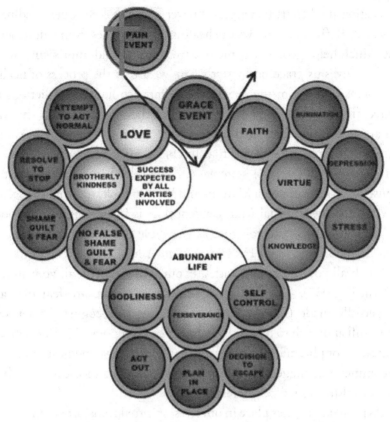

Figure 15. GHP at work: becoming refined

Helping people overcome what they have learned from their broken past into the full revelation Christ has been sent to establish is now possible. A person must be taken from where they are and brought to a place that can have "the faith" established. By being humble and being in attunement with God, we can approach people where they are and help them to be where God desires—if they choose it. Having a better understanding and knowledge of the effects of abnormal childhood experiences helps determine the cause of those maladaptive processes that keep people captive. Prescribed medications are sometimes given with the intention of helping individuals achieve control over a chemical imbalance and provide mental stability, which can be a good thing in the interim. I have discovered that not all medication works, because the individual's emotional problems are not really being recognized, resolved, or addressed.

Medication used to treat symptoms never fixes the core issues needing to be healed. Refinement allows the healing of core issues from a destructive past, which helps people become free from stronghold imprisonment.

God gives us grace no matter where we are in the process of healing (Ephesians 5:8). From my experience so far, people with addictions are injured from within; they are prisoners of their own survival thinking and are eventually controlled by their own habits. While attempting to examine the integration of spiritual and physical being, I noticed Marquis and Warren's (2004, 111) statement: "The self is integral; so must be counseling." The approach Marquis and Warren took was from the secular view toward the spiritual (transcendence). It is interesting to note body, soul, and mind coming together as the Bible describes and commands in Deuteronomy 6. "And He said to him, 'You shall love the Lord your God with all your heart and with all your soul and with all your mind'" (Matthew 22:37). The full recognition of how we are fearfully and wonderfully made (Psalm 139:14) enables us to recognize that people need a full approach to have full healing, not a temporary fix through self-medication or pharmaceutical means. I am not against medication, nor do I recommend or suggest anyone come off prescribed medication without first consulting a medical professional.

As refinement takes place in our lives, spiritual transformation follows. With our growth and maturity in Christ, we become empowered by faith, hope, and love. Greater grace increases our capacity for loving individuals with the realization that God is still working on everyone, even us. As a result, individuals have greater resilience and strength.

– 11 –

Worldwide Epidemics of Anxiety and Depression; Post-Traumatic Stress

For years, there have been reports from several sources showing the progressive increase of anxiety and depression around the world. As an example, the Global Burden of Diseases, Injuries, and Risk Factors Study (GBD) in 2019 showed that the two most disabling mental disorders were depressive and anxiety disorders, both ranked among the top twenty-five leading causes of burden worldwide in 2019.

Currently, anxiety and depression levels have risen dramatically due to world events like COVID-19, and the ramifications for the long term are of concern for everyone. The good news is solutions for finding peace are available. GHP is helping people realign, come out of reactive living or survival mode, and enter a thriving modality. Regaining personal control by entering the peace that surpasses understanding helps individuals see more accurately and becomes a stabilizing force the world needs.

Is PTSD really a diagnosable illness, or is it just sinful worry as some propose? As a side note, it is more appropriate to recognize that post-traumatic stress is not a disorder; the brain is doing what it was designed to do to survive another day. Complex post-traumatic stress disorder is recognized, yet where to place it in the world of diagnosis is being debated. Because there has been a need to address multiple stressful events, some have suggested using the term *disorders of extreme stress not otherwise specified* (DESNOS) as a subcategory of PTSD. Let us examine some of the ramifications of complex PTSD.

WHAT IS COMPLEX PTSD?

Korn (2009) reported that there was a high rate of comorbidity between PTSD and other psychiatric disorders, coupled with an increasingly apparent limitation of DSM-IV TR. The PTSD criteria workgroup studied the existing research literature on trauma and children, female domestic violence victims, and concentration camp survivors. The working group discovered twenty-seven core symptoms that were seen across these different groups and recommended a proposal for a new diagnostic category, referred to as disorders of extreme stress not otherwise specified (DESNOS), also known and referred to as complex PTSD. To justify the addition, the *DSM-IV* implemented field trials studying 400 traumatized individuals seeking treatment and 128 community residents. Field trials found those exposed to prolonged interpersonal trauma, particularly begun at an early age, consistently presented with alterations or dysregulation in seven distinct areas: (a) regulation of effects and impulses, (b) attention or consciousness, (c) self-perception, (d) perception of the perpetrator, (e) relations with others, (f) systems of meaning, and (g) somatization (Korn 2009).

Elbert and Dyck (2004) argued the need for further defining complex PTSD because there were more underlying problems, which they called "complex trauma syndrome." The idea is that exposure to extreme interpersonal stress, exemplified by the experience of torture, represents a threat to the psychological integrity of the victim. The experience is likely to result in mental death, in the loss of the victim's pre-trauma identity. Mental death is characterized by loss of core beliefs and values, distrust, alienation from others, shame and guilt, and a sense of being permanently damaged. Because the core of the person is damaged, mental death is more challenging to treat because of trust issues. Elbert and Dyck (2004) found that the usual approach to treating individuals with complex trauma by using exposure therapy was problematic because of a lack of trust and a refusal to go back to address the event. The individual remains in an emotional state of denial and avoidance.

Mental death is an interesting way to describe chronic trauma, which explains the difficulty in treating certain individuals with post-traumatic stress (PTS) symptoms. A generic diagnosis and treatment of PTS to process a large number of people quickly may not be well suited for all in question. Those individuals who have other issues relating to previous trauma are now reinforced with another traumatic event. Their mental condition is reinforced by feeling and believing certain realities that cause further disconnect and disassociation.

Other areas of this study identified by Elbert and Dyck (2004) were refugees escaping from totalitarian control. The challenge with diagnosing a refugee with PTS was even though a person would present with several indicators pointing toward PTSD, the criteria for PTSD would not be met because there was no reexperiencing of the trauma event. Refugees have reported indicators of impaired affect regulation, dissociative symptoms, somatic complaints, feelings of ineffectiveness, shame, despair, hopelessness, feeling permanently damaged, a loss of previously sustained beliefs, hostility, social withdrawal, feeling constantly threatened, and impaired relationships (Elbert and Dyck, 2004 619), and have had a noticeable change of personality characteristics that are different from before the events.

Sar (2011) identifies complex PTSD as not merely an individual dominated by an anxious response to a single traumatic event. Instead, Sar found the body of research evidence suggests to clinicians to conceptualize PTSD to be inclusive with "terms of a maladaptive, long-lasting, and multi-dimensional consequence of chronic, early, and interpersonal (developmental) traumatization that is known to be the essence of Complex PTSD" (2). Sar also found cumulative trauma during childhood predicts increasing symptom complexity as an adult. Interestingly, trauma experienced as an adult was not a predictor for complex PTSD.

DSM-IV described symptoms of DESNOS (complex PTSD) as follows:

> Impaired affect modulation, self-destructive and impulsive behavior, dissociative symptoms, somatic complaints, feelings of ineffectiveness, shame, despair, or hopelessness, feeling permanently damaged, a loss of previously sustained beliefs, hostility, social withdrawal, feeling constantly threatened, impaired relationships with others, or a change from the individual's previous personality characteristics. (American Psychiatric Association 1994)

While this may be true in a challenging environment for developmental circumstances, those who have been systematically tortured may have symptoms relating to complex PTSD as an adult, according to Elbert and Dyck (2004). Elbert and Dyck found the set of symptoms known as torture syndrome is not specific to the experience of torture. However, it is common among people exposed to any more or less extreme form of totalitarian control. There is an observed relationship between totalitarian control and a complex form of PTSD among adult survivors of severe childhood abuse or domestic violence.

CASE STUDY

Here is one case that is very representative of complex PTSD (CPTSD). A female veteran in her mid-thirties suffers from emotional disconnect and avoidance. Interaction with her children is noted as fragmented and dissociative at best. During an intake interview, they discovered a long history of multiple traumas from childhood, prior to experiencing multiple combat-related traumas while in the army: the loss of her father at three and a half years old, followed by sexual assault by an adult caregiver at four years old, followed by another sexual assault by an adolescent at age six. At age seven, she disclosed the sexual assaults that had occurred. While the perpetrators were being addressed (taken away), her family did not take her to receive any psychiatric or counseling treatment, believing they could simply talk with her if she needed. It was shortly afterward that her mother began taking pills prescribed by a doctor for her nerves. Interestingly, as an adult, she learned her mother was also sexually assaulted and molested when she was around the same age (four to six years old). The family environment she grew up in was with very authoritarian parents and a verbally abusive stepfather. From age fourteen to sixteen, she had a best friend who would take her to church. At age fifteen, she was severely depressed and contemplated suicide. The school counselor quickly referred her for help, and a psychiatrist wanted to place her on medication. Then there was a sexual advance by her best friend's father when she was sixteen. When she got older, she joined the army and had several deployments to different combat zones.

When asked about whether she had any previous treatment, she said she had other counselors who attempted a trauma narrative, however, she did not complete treatment because she "did not feel as she was getting help." The dynamics of her relationship with her husband were chaotic at best, but once there was understanding about how trauma was creating the behaviors, there was greater understanding, and greater communication was experienced. Individual sessions were used with her to help address personal trauma issues, and her husband also had sessions to learn new communication skills to help deescalate tensions.

The purpose of this case was to show that there are many layers of trauma that make it challenging to find resolve. The idea that some people have—"What's your problem? Just get over it and move on! Quit thinking about it!"—is not realistic for the individual experiencing symptoms of trauma. Shaming or guilting someone in these types of situations is counterproductive and helps create post-traumatic church disorder (PTCD).

The challenge of treating CPTSD is developing a counseling relationship because of past issues interfering with the development of trust. Chu (2011) relays that when neglect and hurt come from within the structure of the family, the child learns to mirror the parents' reaction and response to the trauma event. Chu reports that the resultant effect is they have learned to approach relationships (including therapeutic) with others with a deep mistrust; relationships translate as being tenuous and dangerous at best. In addressing CPTSD, the idea expressed by Tick (2005), about the self-identity being destroyed, is supported through an ignored disclosure by parents in situations previously mentioned. The challenge in using trauma-focused cognitive behavioral therapy (TF-CBT) is helping the parents work through their own issues of trauma as the children develop their personal narratives. I have been a proponent of TF-CBT and have been appreciative of its development, but in actual use I found it limiting when working with individuals with complex PTSD. Simple trauma is perhaps a one-time incident, whereas more complex issues have fragmented and displaced cognitive abilities.

The narrative approach cannot reach the rest of the brain's memory because of the way trauma is being stored. The rewriting of the narrative helps cognitive function, but the rest of the mind and body remembers. This has been an issue in treating people, whether they are veterans coming back from forward-deployed assignments or individuals who have grown up in their own hostile home environments. "Talking about it" depends upon an individual's memory of events that are not accurate because of the brain's processing design as individuals experience trauma. The services given by Veterans Affairs that she received were mostly remediation of symptoms using medications. This is just one example of trauma issues in an individual's experience. The application of GHP in the case study was also having to include and deal with post-traumatic church disorder (PTCD) to establish connectivity back to God.

At a children's advocacy center, I discovered several cases of children who experienced sexual abuse. When the parents were encouraged to seek counseling services for themselves, it was discovered they had their own child sexual abuse history that had never been treated. To be exact, I discovered that 90 percent of the parents had issues growing up with exposure to domestic violence, experiencing physical and emotional abuse directly. Seventy percent of those affected parents reported being sexually abused without ever receiving treatment. The questions and guilt around the helplessness and failed personal expectations that they should be able to protect their children from such abusive situations were devastating. Sadly, when I applied for funding or grants to treat these parents who had experienced sexual abuse as children, it was never granted.

Another area where I noticed trauma was when I was working in an opiate addiction clinic. It was a medicated assisted treatment (MAT) program that used primarily methadone for the treatment of addiction. The predominant theme was viewing opiate addiction as a disease that needed to be treated like diabetes. I had a caseload of 130 people, and there was a reoccurring theme for those coming in for treatment. I found 90 percent of my clients had complex PTS from childhood. Some asked for a faith-based approach, and I used GHP principles and discovered nearly all of them had post-traumatic church disorder (PTCD). The most common response received after showing GHP to them was, "Wow, this makes sense! Why aren't the churches talking about it?" A few of my clients became stable enough to leave the clinic without abusing substances anymore. When I realized how many people had complex trauma issues, I spoke to the counseling director, explaining the predominance of trauma that may likely be creating addictive behavior. I asked, "Why are we putting

Band-Aids on bullet holes?" The director responded, "Here, we only treat substance abuse disorders. Trauma issues are given a referral to another facility." It was a good learning experience that gave greater understanding and shaped my approach to the dynamics of trauma treatment.

SOME BIBLICAL EXAMPLES OF PTSD

Many people have their idea of control shattered when they experience traumatic events. Is there biblical evidence supporting whether there is such a thing as PTSD (aka PTS)?

Adam and Eve were the first couple to experience multiple episodes of PTS. The first case was being before God and facing the consequences of eating from the tree of the knowledge of good and evil. The directive that was in place was to eat from the tree would be their death. The second time would be with the murder of their son Abel by their son Cain. This created further separation from the family because Cain continued until his death to go from place to place without having a home (Genesis 3–5).

Luger (2012) discusses three characters from the Bible who had to deal with PTS. The first was Noah in Genesis 6. Noah's righteousness is noted in his characterization and in his actions. Noah demonstrated loyalty and acceptance of God's commandment by the building of an ark, which took more than 120 years. After all the animals were gathered into the ark and Noah was joined by his family, they witnessed the complete annihilation of all known civilization. Luger (2012) points out that Jewish literature is replete with narratives of how burdensome life on the ark was for Noah. When Noah emerged from the ark, he was no longer the same Noah that had gone aboard the ark a year earlier. Luger suggests that Noah was not the same righteous man but a broken man. The evidence given was the first thing Noah did was plant a vineyard and get drunk. Luger noted it is not surprising that Noah turns to alcohol—a common outlet for patients with PTS. In this case, Luger makes the point that Noah was notably affected by his trauma.

There are two other cases Luger brings out. First is where Lot's wife saw the destruction of Sodom and Gomorrah. Lot and his daughters escaped the destruction of Sodom and Gomorrah. However, Lot lost his wife, and the daughters lost their fiancés. Luger describes how Lot's wife metaphorically becomes "a pillar of salt" (Genesis 19:26), a catatonic reaction to stress. The idea is she became as immobile and rigid as a pillar of salt or frozen. This is a catatonic reaction, which has been described in the psychiatric literature because of severe psychological trauma. Luger then brings out how Abraham's son, Isaac, was nearly sacrificed by his father but saved by an angel of God. Luger points out that this is the only character written in the Torah who is incapable of finding his own spouse. Luger's speculation was, Did the trauma Isaac experienced leave him untrusting and withdrawn? The double trauma that Isaac went through was his own experience of nearly being killed by his father as a sacrifice and the loss of his mother. Luger makes the point that whereas Noah and Lot's wife were destroyed by PTS, Isaac found recovery through connection with his wife (Genesis 24:67) and reassurance from God (Genesis 26:3).

Jonah

After witnessing and knowing about different atrocities that the Nineveh had done to Israel and other nations, Jonah was told to tell them that God wants them to repent, or they will be destroyed. Jonah displays cultural systemic traumatization, wanting to avoid God's mercy toward Nineveh. Then Jonah suffers further trauma by being thrown off the boat and being swallowed by the whale. After delivering the message, Nineveh repents, and Jonah suffers further self-induced trauma due to what his system of belief was based on, which was by vengeance being rendered instead of mercy. Jonah had his own desired outcome (or stronghold) in mind instead of God's will.

Job

The book of Job demonstrates the epitome of human trauma and resilience. Briefly stated, Job's affliction wiped out his family and possessions, his health was taken, and his wife turned against him. Even the friends who came to comfort him falsely accused him of having sinned against God. Despite the trauma, pain, and disappointments Job had in life, there was a greater hope because it was recognized who was ultimately in control. Job had arguments with God about everything but eventually came to realize the truth.

> Then Job answered the LORD and said: "I know that you can do all things, and that no purpose of yours can be thwarted. 'Who is this that hides counsel without knowledge?' Therefore I have uttered what I did not understand, things too wonderful for me, which I did not know. 'Hear, and I will speak; I will question you, and you make it known to me.' I had heard of you by the hearing of the ear, but now my eye sees you; therefore I despise myself, and repent in dust and ashes." (Job 42:1–6)

Unger (1984, 216) stated, "Job's reply to God solves the problem of suffering, Job 42:1–6. Affliction is God-permitted to refine man so that he may see God, 5, in all His greatness and splendor, and see himself in his despicableness and sin to the intent that men may repent of his pride 'in dust and ashes.'" Crabb (2001) even explores the idea of longsuffering and the result of God's intent in using it for good.

Jesus Christ

Jesus suffered multiple trauma events before he was executed. Part of the speculation is that Jesus's earthly father, Joseph, had died, leaving Jesus to take care of Mary until His other siblings could take over the family business. He was betrayed by a close friend, deserted by everyone, beaten, accused, mocked, and flogged. He was mad, disappointed, and in anguish, crying out to God as He hung on the cross (Matthew 27:46). "My God, My God, why have You forsaken me?" (Mark 15:34 ESV). Yet after all the traumatic experiences, He rose from the grave to give hope, comfort, and faith in what lays beyond this life. Jesus also told us that we will experience similar trials in this life and should not be surprised when they occur.

The song "Ten Thousand Angels" (Overholt 1959) describes what Jesus could have done had He chosen (Matthew 26:53), but He continued doing His Father's will instead of His own (Matthew 26:39, 42). For those who truly experience trauma from people from whom you would believe it should never come, consider that Jesus was also rejected by those He came to save. A person who experiences this type of trauma (PTSD) can greatly appreciate what Jesus did, knowing that if the choice were left to them, the end results would be different. This perspective allows for a greater understanding and appreciation of God's grace through Christ.

COMBAT VETERANS

Combat stresses leave invisible wounds that go unrecognized because a person seems normal on the outside. Besides PTSD, traumatic brain injury (TBI) can result from blunt-force trauma from various factors such as improvised explosive devices or vehicle accidents. Combat veterans have greater exposure to TBI due to the nature of military service. Individuals with TBI experience disruption of synaptic systems in the brain, which interferes with everyday living—what they knew they could once do and remember, and even memories about their family history, are displaced. Tick (2005) proposes that combatants also have their sense of self, established in civilian life, shattered. Tick takes a Jungian approach to PTSD. The idea is that an individual without the direction of understanding and integrating their experiences within a moral context is lost in a mythical state. Not having a way for pulling together the two sides leaves combatants trapped in the realm of war itself unable to cope in the civilian world. Tick considers the essence of PTSD to be more like "an identity disorder" (5). This contrasts with other conceptualizations that the brain simply has a stress regulation mechanism gone awry. If we fail to honor an individual's experience, we magnify a state of dis-ease within.

McKelvey (2009) made observations of veterans who had started out with a faith in God only to find it being questioned after coming home from Afghanistan and Iraq. The question was raised whether faith-based interventions were effective or only hindering progress that needed to be accomplished. The military distributed a book by Rick Warren called *The Purpose Driven Life*, and different groups used a type of group therapy approach to help service members. This book offered hope but was not a fix-all, in that there were members of the military who committed suicide because of stressors and unrelieved trauma issues. During that time, the purpose behind the mission in Iraq was in error because no weapons of mass destruction were found. For some, the misplaced trust of Christian military members meant their faith in government was placed above their faith in God. In Romans 13:1–8, Paul talks to the Christians about being obedient to governing authorities because God has put them in place for a reason. The challenge comes from the understanding that even though the context of war may be justified by humans, God's larger intention is carried out even though it is not always understood by those carrying it through (1 Peter 1:10–12).

There are some like Zelmer (2011) who have called PTSD a part of our sinful nature. Zelmer considered two options: one is the path to death, and the other is the path to life. He addressed the stigma of the label of the PTSD identity, saying that any sin committed will be magnified in their minds and the PTSD will tell them to give up, to enter despair, to kill themselves. The PTSD identity will want us to feel always and fully alienated from our relationships. This is because the way of PTSD is the way of death (Zelmer 2011). Zelmer recognizes the thought process involved and the need to identify whether the guilt felt is reasonable and honest, thus warranting change. The need to become self-destructive using substances (whether they are legal or illegal) will not be a solution to healing from within. As far as addressing reoccurring flashbacks and unprovoked intrusive thoughts that are beyond an individual's free will choice, Zelmer gave no solutions in his article. Zelmer's article was refuted by many individuals and is no longer available. I extend God's grace toward Zelmer and those who do not know or understand God's design. The brain's design is for survival to help us stay alive another day, but that leads to existing in survival mode.

In contrast to Zelmer's views, I submit that which is evident but rarely noticed. Our salvation is based in trauma! This shows that beyond the pain we experience, greater love exists. God's healing process continues throughout life for those who are ready for healing. GHP has helped many people and will continue to help many more. Why not you, and why not now?

BRAINSPOTTING

Brainspotting is one of my favorite tools to use when helping individuals with trauma issues. Why? Because it works! Many military combat veterans do not want to relive or tell their stories to other individuals outside of their group. Brainspotting allows the processing of events in the subcortical area of the brain without having to talk about it. Brainspotting is a useful technique for you if you have worked on yourself for a while and feel you still can't shift something that is keeping you blocked.

When we go through a trauma in life, we naturally react with fight, flight, or freeze. When we freeze, a connection between the feelings we had at the time of trauma and a feeling in our body occurs. That stuck-frozen feeling becomes formatted within us and reoccurs when we encounter similar situations with new challenges. Often to create a new way of approaching life more harmoniously, we need to complete the movement that did not happen in the original trauma.

Brainspotting allows your body to release the stress that it learned in the past. This focused attention on a situation seems to trigger deep in our brain the area that contains unprocessed memory and feeling. It appears to tap into our own body's innate wisdom to heal. It has the potential to unlock the circular thinking, negative thoughts, self-protective patterns, and limiting beliefs we continuously act from even when we don't want to.

I have had a great deal of success in working with individuals dealing with trauma utilizing Brainspotting techniques. Those whom I have helped asked to have their stories shared with the GHP process. Although there are several, I selected two individuals to illustrate the progress they made. Names will be abbreviated for confidentiality reasons.

JM

During a combat women's retreat held by a Special Forces–aligned organization, I gave my introductory presentation about GHP, called "Finding Peace in a World Without." By invitation, I arrived an hour and a half early to meet and talk over supper with the women there for the retreat. That was where I met JM. She was withdrawn from the group, and her disposition was heavily guarded. I engaged in conversation with her, and she responded and became more receptive. During the presentation, I spoke about Brainspotting and the results I noticed in my private practice. Because of the group interest, I asked JM if she would like to try Brainspotting because I recognized issues she was carrying, and because of our conversation before the presentation, I had developed a level of safety and trust. She agreed, and I did the setup with her frame on the helicopter's collision and crash that killed several team members she was in command of while returning from a mission.

Using the pointer, I was able to recognize a point of emotional access (outside window, with somatic recognition), and she began processing for around fifty minutes. Afterward, she mentioned being tired but also having a greater level of peace. During the session, physical tensions were released that had been stored at the subcortical level. JM was surprised and even noticed good memories that had been suppressed. "I remember thinking how beautiful the sunset was that day." The next day at the retreat, everyone noticed the transformational change she had undergone; she was smiling and engaging with everyone. We continued further sessions past the retreat, and she made transformational progress, including quitting drinking. She also left an unsolicited review:

> Caveat: Before you read this review, I am a firm believer like dentists, lawyers, and financial advisors ... doctors are an extremely personal decision. Not every doctor is going to fit every personality, nor should it. That said, I fully admit before I met Dr. Copeland, I was in a lot of pain. Was in pain for over a decade. Lacked trust in all people with titles that started with the letters *psych*. Dr. Copeland convinced me I was wrong. Below is my humble opinion:
>
> There is nothing more to say other than compared to over ten VA therapists in four separate hospitals over the last fifteen years ... Hallelujah, we finally found someone who actually gets it!
>
> Front Office Support—Phenomenal!
>
> Dreeta [Copeland] ... Amazing! Ten out of ten!

Telecare Support—Love that Dr. Copeland offers this option. This is really important as family schedules get hectic.

For veterans who have seen and been through multiple traumas, multiple TBIs, and multiple accidents, and who have physical and mental pain points ... Dr. Copeland is your doctor to talk to. He offers many types of healing modalities. If you hate medicines or trying to stop taking medicines, perhaps he can help you as he has helped our family. He is a man who has life experience and combat experience, truly listens to the patient, and doesn't give you those typical responses that make you want to puke: "How does that make you feel?" "Well, you have to put in the work to see progress ..." Blah, blah, blah. No patronizing here. Thank goodness!

Dr. Copeland doesn't make a combat veteran feel ashamed or relive the trauma over and over again, which some believe will magically make veterans feel better. Maybe this works for some? Hasn't worked in our household. Just makes us angrier, and we never go back. We love talking to Dr. Copeland because he has a way to draw out those memories without creating more pain and more anger. The best way to describe it is that he mentors, coaches, and guides us to heal our own pain. He helps us understand where and why we are in so much pain. While it may sound intuitive, everyone needs that one special person who believes in you, who can coach you. For us, that is Dr. Copeland. He offers humor when you need it. He offers his ear when you need it. He offers mentorship when you may not want it but absolutely need it.

He is a busy, busy man! So for those of us who need him or refer him to those in need, please, please cancel your appointment early so someone else can have the appointment. He is truly a precious commodity that needs to be shared.

AK

AK was a referral from one of the veterans and special forces organizations to come to counseling. His PTSD issues were disruptive in his relationships with his girlfriend and her daughter. While serving in Afghanistan, he witnessed several brutal acts of violence including a suicide bomber who detonated themselves in an area with many children. His unit had been working and interacting with the children. After doing some remote work with Brainspotting, he was less driven (reactive) and able to be more present with his relationships. Using the GHP principles, he was able to have better alignment in love than being driven by fear, gaining a greater resilience while even facing false allegations. His release of vengeance and anger allowed him to enter a greater place of peace. He gave me his full experience of GHP and the trials he went through, but I will not share every detail.

> God's healing process is an opportunity for you to heal from your past trauma and situations, and to look up to God for redemption to have a realignment to God to receive the blessings God has waiting for you. I feel alive, more than ever before ... I have been released from the master of revenge and brought into the Prince of Peace.

IN CONCLUSION

There is no shortage of people who are hurting and have experienced trauma. An accurate description of the world could be summed up as systemic traumatization. That is, hurt people continue to hurt people because they were done wrong. Instead of letting go, forgiving, and being able to move beyond the pain of the past, they continue in fearful expectation of the same continued trauma events. Vengeance and revenge become dark themes in people's lives. They stay captive by fear and prejudge others by the expectations they were taught to believe, in a way that could be called secondary or generational systemic traumatization. There is no denying that there have been traumatic events done by people in the past. It is not about race but about God's grace.

God's healing process was something I needed in my own life. I also found many others who were hurting and disconnected from God in their lives. They had a religion but no spiritual transformation. I had a long delay in publishing this book, but I have had a lot of support and encouragement from those who testify that GHP has made a difference in their life and made a positive impact on their families.

I am glad that God has given us all different talents and abilities that we can use to further His kingdom. If we develop and use our talents accordingly, God will use each of us by His design in wonderfully magnificent ways. There may be times of personal disappointment, and there may be times of great success. Regardless, God gets the glory in all things. So, are you walking in darkness or in the light?

LIST OF FIGURES

Figure 1. Behavioral cycle (Wilkins 2006) 20
Figure 2. God's healing process theory 31
Figure 3. Open hand (A) and closed fist (B) examples 35
Figure 4. God's healing process (Copeland 2011). 37
Figure 5. Behavior Cycle (Wilkins 2006) 50
Figure 6. God's Healing Process (Copeland, 2011) 51
Figure 7. Pain cycle results 52
Figure 8. Whitewashed tombs 52
Figure 9. Fruit of Spirit naturally manifested 54
Figure 10. Spiritual living denies fleshly desires 54
Figure 11. GHP Christian developmental cycle 65
Figure 12. GHP Christian developmental cycle, continued 66
Figure 13. Pain Event Cycle within Creation Therapy 69
Figure 14. God's Healing Process within Creation Therapy 70
Figure 15. GHP at work: becoming refined 85

REFERENCES

Scripture quotations are from the Holy Bible, English Standard Version, copyright © 2001 by Crossway Bibles, a publishing ministry of Good News Publishers. Used by permission. All rights reserved.

Amen, D. 2015. *Change Your Brain, Change Your Life.* 10th ed. New York: Harmony.

Jean Arno, R., and P. Jean Arno. 1993. *Creation Therapy: A Biblically Based Model for Christian Counseling.* Unknown Binding.

Awad, F. 2010. "Pornography Addiction: A Cognitive Approach in Combating the Lies Christian Males Believe." Thesis project submitted to Liberty Baptist Theological Seminary. http://www.liberty.edu.ezproxy.liberty.edu: 2048/informationservices/ilrc/library/.

Blue Letter Bible. 1996. "Dictionary and Word Search in the NIV." *Blue Letter Bible.* http://www.blueletterbible.org/search/translationResults.

Blue Letter Bible. 2011. "Dictionary and Word Search." *Blue Letter Bible.* 1996–2011. http://www.blueletterbible.org/lang/lexicon/Lexicon.cfm.

Bostwick, M., and J. Bucci. 2008. "Internet Sex Addiction Treated with Naltrexone." *Mayo Clinic Proceedings* 83, no. 2: 226. http://www.liberty.edu.ezproxy.liberty.edu:2048/informationservices/ilrc/library/.

Bufford, R. K. 1997. "Consecrated Counseling: Reflections on the Distinctive of Christian Counseling." *Journal of Psychology and Theology* 31, no. 1: 24–36.

Carnes, P. 1992. *Don't Call It Love: Recovery from Sexual Addiction.* New York: Bantam.

Carnes, P., and K. Adams. 2002. *Clinical Management of Sex Addiction*. New York: Taylor, Francis.

Chu, J. 2011. *Rebuilding Shattered Lives: Treating Complex PTSD and Dissociative Disorders*. Hoboken, NJ: John Wiley and Sons

Clinton, T., and G. Ohlschlager. 2006. *Competent Christian Counseling, Vol. 1*. Colorado Springs, CO: WaterBrook.

Cloitre, M., C. Courtois, A. Charuvastra, R. Carapezza, B. Stolbach, and B. Green. 2011. "Treatment of Complex PTSD: Results of the ISTSS Expert Clinician Survey on Best Practices." *Journal of Traumatic Stress* 24, no. 6. http://onlinelibrary.wiley.com.ezproxy.liberty.edu:2048/doi/10.1002/jts.20697/pdf.

Crabb, L. 1977. *Effective Biblical Counseling: A Model for Helping Caring Christians Become Capable Counselors*. Grand Rapids, MI: Zondervan.

Davis, J. 1992. Dictionary of the Bible. 4th ed. Old Tappan, NJ: Fleming H. Revell.

D'Urso, A., and J. H. Brickner. 2014. "Mechanisms of Epigenetic Memory." *Trends in Genetics* 30, no. 6: 230–236. https://doi.org/10.1016/j.tig.2014.04.004.

Dyslin, C. W. 2008. "The Power of Powerlessness: The Role of Spiritual Surrender and Interpersonal Confession in the Treatment of Addictions." *Journal of Psychology and Christianity* 27, no. 1: 41–56.

Easton, M. G. 2007. *Easton's Bible Dictionary*. http://www.blueletterbible.org/Search/Dictionary/viewTopic.cfm?type=GetTopic&Topic=Wise,+Wisdom&DictList=2#Easton's.

Edward, T. 2005. *War and the Soul*. Wheaton, IL: Quest.

Elbert, A., and M. Dyck. 2004. "The Experience of Mental Death: The Core Feature of Complex Post-Traumatic Stress Disorder." *Clinical Psychology Review* 24:617–635.

Garzon, F., and K. Tilley. 2009. "Do Lay Christian Counseling Approaches Work? What We Currently Know." *Journal of Psychology and Christianity* 28, no. 2: 130–140.

GBD. 2019. Disease and Injuries Collaborators: Global Burden of 369 Diseases and Injuries in 204 Countries and Territories, 1990–2019: A Systematic Analysis for the Global Burden of Disease Study 2019. *Lancet* 396:1204–1222.

Guzik, D. 2006a. "Study Guide for Colossians." *Enduring Word*. http://www.blueletterbible.org/commentaries/comm_view.cfm?AuthorID=2&contentID=8044&commInfo=31&topic=Colossians&r=Col_2_3.

Guzik, D. 2006b. "Study Guide for Galatians 5." *Enduring Word*. http://www.blueletterbible.org/commentaries/comm_view.cfm?AuthorID=2&contentID=8031&commInfo=31&topic=Galatians&ar=Gal_5_23.

Guzik, D. 2006c. "Study Guide for 1 Peter 2." *Enduring Word*. http://www.blueletterbible.org/commentaries/comm_view.cfm?AuthorID=2&contentID=8088&commInfo=31&topic=1%20Peter&ar=1Pe_2_11.

Henry, M. 1996a. "Commentary on 1 Kings 12." https://www.blueletterbible.org/Comm/mhc/1Ki/1Ki_012.cfm.

Henry, M. 1996b. "Commentary on Proverbs 20." http://www.blueletterbible.org/commentaries/comm_view.cfm?AuthorID=4&contentID=1294&commInfo=5&topic=Proverbs&ar=Pro_20_1.

Henry, M. 1996c. "Commentary of Isaiah 5." http://www.blueletterbible.org/commentaries/comm_view.cfm?AuthorID=4&contentID=1333&commInfo=5&topic=Isaiah&ar=Isa_5_22.

Hester, R. K., and W. R. Miller. 2003. *Handbook of Alcoholism Treatment Approaches: Effective Alternatives*. 3rd ed. Boston: Pearson Education.

Hook, Joshua, and Jan Hook. 2010. "The Healing Cycle: A Christian Model for Group Therapy." *Journal of Psychology and Christianity* 29, no. 4: 308–316. http://www.liberty.edu.ezproxy.liberty.edu:2048/informationservices/ilrc/library/.

Horton, D. 2009. "Discerning Spiritual Discernment: Assessing Current Approaches for Understanding God's Will." *Journal of Youth Ministry* 7, no. 2: 7–31. http://web.ebscohost.com.ezproxy.liberty.edu:2048/ehost/detail?hid=17&sid=370499c3-5973-46e1-8018-4847379cb927%40sessionmgr4&vid=1&bdata=JnNpdGU9ZWhvc3QtbGl2ZSZzY29wZT1zaXRl#db=a9h&AN=38605763.

Korn, D. 2009. "EMDR and the Treatment of Complex PTSD: A Review." *Journal of EMDR Practice and Research* 3, no. 4: 264

Ksir, C., C. Hart, and O. Ray. 2011. *Drugs, Society, and Human Behavior*. 14th ed. Boston: McGraw-Hill.

Luger, S. 2010. "Flood, Salt, and Sacrifice: Post-Traumatic Stress Disorders in Genesis." *Jewish Bible Quarterly* 38, no. 2: 124.

Marquis, A., and S. Warren. 2004. "Integral Counseling." *Constructivism in the Human Sciences* 9, no. 1: 111.

Martin, R. P. "2 Corinthians" In *Word Biblical Commentary*, vol. 40. Waco, TX: Word, 1986, 306.

McClone, K. 2003. "Psycospirituality of Addiction." *Seminary Journal Cornwell University* 9 (Winter): 26–33. https://www.issmcclone.com/pblctns/psychospirituality_addiction.pdf.

McKelvey, T. 2009. "God, the Army, and PTSD: Is Religion an Obstacle to Treatment?" *Boston Review* 34, no. 6: 22.

Miller, W. R. 1995. "Toward a Biblical Perspective on Drug Use." *Journal of Ministry in Addiction and Recovery* 2, no. 2: 77–86.

Miller W. R, and E. Kurtz. 1994. "Models of Alcoholism Used in Treatment: Contrasting AA and Other Perspectives with Which It Is Often Confused." *J Stud Alcohol* 55 (2): 159–66. doi:10.15288/jsa.1994.55.159.

Neff, J. A., C. T. Shorkey, and L. C. Windsor. 2006. "Contrasting Faith-Based and Traditional Substance Abuse Treatment Programs." *Journal of Substance Abuse Treatment* 30:49–61.

Orr, J. 2007. "Help." *International Standard Bible Encyclopaedia*. http://www.blueletterbible.org/Search/Dictionary /viewTopic.cf type=GetTopic.

Ortberg, J. 2005. *God Is Closer Than You Think*. Grand Rapids, MI: Zondervan.

Pandya, S. 2011 "Understanding Brain, Mind and Soul: Contributions from Neurology and Neurosurgery." *Brain, Mind and Consciousness* 9, no. 1: 129–149.

Roberts, A., and G. Koob. 1997. "The Neurobiology of Addiction." *Alcohol Health and Research World* 21, no. 2. http://www.liberty.edu.ezproxy.liberty.edu:2048/informationservices/ilrc/library/.

Shaffer, L. 2008. "Religion as a Large-Scale Justification System: Does the Justification Hypothesis Explain Animistic Attribution?" *Theory and Psychology* 18, no. 6: 779–799.

Smith, C. 2005. "Psalm 120–125." *The Word for Today*. http://www.blueletterbible.org/Search/Dictionary/viewTopic.cfm? type=GetTopic.

Strong, J. 1990. *The New Strong's Exhaustive Concordance of the Bible*. Nashville: Thomas Nelson.

Swindoll, C. 1996. *Hope Again: When Life Hurts and Dreams Fade*. Dallas: Word.

Tick, E. 2005. *War and the Soul: Healing Our Nation's Veterans from Post-Traumatic Stress Disorder*. Wheaton, IL: Quest.

Thayer J. 1841. *Thayer's Greek-English Lexicon*. http://www.blueletterbible.org/lang/lexicon/lexicon.cfm?Strongs=G1466&t=KJV.

Unger, M 1984. *The New Unger's Bible Handbook*. Revised by Gary Larson. Chicago: Moody.

Vine, W. E. 2007. *Vine's Expository Dictionary of Biblical Words*. http://www.blueletterbible.org/Search/Dictionary /viewTopic.cfm?type=GetTopic&Topic=Counsel&DictList=9# Vine's.

Vine, W. E. 1985. *Vine's Expository Dictionary of Biblical Words*. Nashville: Thomas Nelson.

Wehrenberg, M. **2016.** "Rumination: A Problem in Anxiety and Depression Springboard Out of Negative Networks into New Solutions." *Psychology Today*, April 20. https://www.psychologytoday.com/blog/depression-management-techniques/201604/rumination-problem-in-anxiety-and-depression.

Wilkins, R. 2006. *Removing Emotional Pain*. 1st ed. La Vergne, TN: SFT Awareness.

Zelmer, J. 2011. "Judas, Peter, and Choosing the Right Path." *PTSD Spirituality: Healing Souls Wounded by PTSD.* http://www.ptsdspirituality.com/2011/08/24/ptsd-spirituality-judas-peter-and-choosing-the-right-path/.

Zinnabauer, B. J., and K. I. Pargament. 2000. "Working with the Sacred: Four Approaches to Religious and Spiritual Issues in Counseling." *Journal of Counseling and Development* 78: 162–171.

Godshealingprocess.com